W9-BVC-905

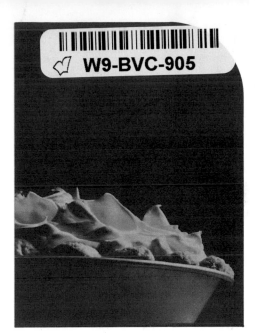

pillsbury publications

Pillsbury's Bake Off Dessert Cook Book

Shortcutted prize winning favorites...the best of all the 'Bake Offs

Dear Homemaker,

There are times when the first word spoken
at the family dinner table (usually by a
younger member) is, "What's for dessert?"
Does that sound familiar?

Hot or cold, simple or elaborate, dessert
is the climax of an enjoyable meal. It is
something sweet and special, withheld until
the last to heighten the anticipation.

Eighteen years of Pillsbury Bake Offs have
brought to us from all over the country the
best recipes for most-loved desserts, as
well as some new twists on old favorites
and some deliciously original ideas. They
include everything from good-tasting standbys
for family suppers to special occasion
beauties for showing off.

We have taken a choice selection and brought
them up to date with short-cuts and the use
of convenience food ingredients, where
possible. With each recipe, you'll find
short descriptions to help you quickly
visualize the finished pie or dessert.

Of all the foods you prepare for your family,
they probably will cheer you most for
your desserts. We hope you try many from
this collection . . . perhaps make one
or more of them your specialty.

Cordially yours,

Ann Pillsbury

Copyright © 1968 by the Pillsbury Company. Printed in U.S.A.
Second Printing 1971

Contents

Basics

All about . . .

Flour keeps best in a covered canister. If you store it in the bag, keep it tightly covered. Pillsbury's Best All Purpose Flour has been used in developing the recipes in this book. To measure flour, simply spoon it lightly into your measuring cup and level it off with the straight edge of a spatula or knife.

Butter or margarine are called for in many of the recipes in this book. These recipes will work with either butter or margarine; however, do keep in mind that butter will add a special flavor and richness. Some recipes call for butter or margarine, softened. It is essential that the butter or margarine has a chance to warm to room temperature (about 70°) in order to blend in with the other ingredients. Do not confuse whipped butter or margarine. Since these are whipped and volume is increased, special adjustments must be made when using them in cooking and baking. Some brands give the special recipe adjustments. You will notice with the whipped margarine that there are 6 sticks in a pound instead of the usual 4 and that each stick contains ⅓ cup for recipe use rather than the usual ½ cup.

Eggs should be stored in the refrigerator as they will deteriorate rapidly with warm temperatures. Be sure the eggs you buy have been refrigerated, then leave them in the carton and store in your refrigerator. Leftover egg whites and egg yolks can be stored, tightly covered, in the refrigerator for up to 2 days. For longer storage, cover tightly and freeze; then allow to thaw in refrigerator. When ready to use, remember that:

1 egg white	=	3 tablespoons
1 egg yolk	=	1 tablespoon
1 egg	=	¼ cup

Eggs are used in some recipes in this book where there is no cooking. Be sure the eggs you use for these recipes are fresh Grade AA eggs and have been refrigerated. It is possible for cracked or dirty shell eggs to contain salmonella bacteria. For this reason whole shell, clean eggs only should be used in making food products that are uncooked. Thorough cooking or baking will destroy this bacteria.

Be sure any egg or custard pie or dessert is stored in the refrigerator as soon as cool. Then, use within 2 days.

Freezing pies and desserts for later use will add variety to your meals as well as save time, especially if your family is small. If you have the time, make up extra and freeze for later use or if the recipe makes more than you can use in a few meals, freeze half for later use. Remember, though, that cream (cornstarch thickened) and custard pies curdle and that meringue tends to become tough during freezing. Therefore, avoid freezing pies and desserts with custard or cream-type fillings and meringue toppings.

Fruit pies freeze very well either before baking or after baking. When freezing unbaked pies, wait and slit the top crust just before baking to avoid drying the filling during freezer storage. Unwrap frozen pies, slit top, place in oven as recipe directs allowing 15 to 20 minutes extra time. If pie is baked first, unwrap and allow to thaw several hours or place in 350° oven for thawing in about 30 minutes. The oven warming will give the pie that fresh baked taste and also helps prevent crust sogginess. Chiffon (gelatin) and refrigerated (whipped cream) pies will keep frozen for 2 to 3 weeks. Freeze uncovered until firm, 3 to 4 hours. Wrap tightly and freeze. To thaw, unwrap and place in refrigerator 3 to 4 hours.

Freeze pie shells either baked or unbaked. This is an excellent way to use leftover pastry—and then when you want a pie, the pastry is already made.

Cake and cobbler desserts freeze very nicely. Bake, cool and freeze. If served warm, unwrap and thaw in oven. If cakes are thawed at room temperature, leave wrapped.

When freezing, be sure the food is cool, the wrapping is moisture-vapor proof, all the air is removed and the wrap is air tight. Label and freeze. You're now ready for a quick and easy dessert for family or unexpected company.

Choice of Dessert for Meals—Everyone wonders, "What's for dessert?" Plan your dessert so it will be the perfect climax for your main course. Let desserts help vary your combinations of colors, flavors, textures, temperatures and shapes. If the main course is rich and saucy, keep the dessert light and simple. When the main course is hearty and simple, bring on a rich and luscious dessert. Nothing tastes better after a spicy entree than a cool, refreshing, tart dessert. Yet on a cold winter evening nothing smells and tastes better than a spicy dessert that's warm out of the oven and topped with a mound of cool whipped cream. Have fun, be creative and let your desserts be the perfect finish for your meals.

Terms

Special helps for directions and ingredients used in this book.

Directions:

A la mode . . . To serve with ice cream.

Baste . . . During cooking, or baking, to spoon sauce over.

Blend . . . To combine two or more ingredients thoroughly.

Boil, gently . . . To heat or cook just below the boiling point.

Boil, rolling . . . To heat or cook until bubbles constantly break the surface.

Caramelize . . . To heat sugar until it is melted and browned.

Chill . . . To place in refrigerator or other cold place until cold.

Chop . . . To cut into small pieces.

Coats spoon . . . When custard mixture leaves a thin, even film on metal spoon that has been dipped and allowed to drain.

Cool . . . To let stand at room temperature or in cold water until no longer warm.

Combine . . . To mix together two or more ingredients.

Cream . . . To blend a fat with sugar until light and completely blended.

Cube . . . To cut into small cubes of a regular size.

Cut in . . . To use two knives, pastry blender or fork to distribute shortening through dry ingredients, leaving it in small particles.

Cut up . . . To cut into smaller pieces.

Dice . . . To cut into very small cubes.

Dot . . . To scatter small particles (usually butter) over food.

Flour . . . To cover completely with a thin layer of flour.

Fold . . . To combine delicate ingredients (beaten egg white or whipped cream) without air loss. Insert spatula down through the middle of mixture, across bottom, bring it up and "fold" over onto mixture. Continue until all is evenly mixed.

Glaze . . . To coat with syrup, thin icing or jelly, either during cooking or after the food is cooked.

Grate . . . To rub a food against a grater to form small particles.

Grind . . . To put through a food grinder.

Icing . . . A mixture of sugar and other ingredients, either cooked or uncooked, used to cover a cake or sweet rolls. Frosting.

Knead . . . To work dough by repeatedly stretching it with hands, folding it over and pressing it with knuckles or "heel" of the hand.

Meringue . . . A mixture of stiffly beaten egg whites and sugar baked on top of pies or desserts or as small cakes or shells.

Mince . . . To chop very fine.

Peel . . . To remove peeling or outer covering, usually with knife.

Sauté . . . To cook in a skillet in a small amount of fat.

Scald . . . To heat just below the boiling point. Also to pour boiling water over food or dip food briefly into boiling water.

Shred . . . To tear or cut into thin strips.

Soft mounds . . . To beat mixture until mounds form.

Soft peaks . . . To beat mixture until peaks form that readily bend over.

Steam . . . To cook in the steam of water that is in the vessel below.

Stiff peaks . . . To beat mixture until peaks form and hold their shape.

Toast . . . To brown by direct heat in oven or toaster.

Whip . . . To beat rapidly with rotary or electric mixer to add air and make substance light and fluffy.

Ingredients:

Apple pie slices . . . Apples canned in water, without thickening or spices.

Apple pie filling . . . Prepared apples canned in thickened sauce and spices. Ready to be used in pastry crust.

Almond paste . . . A paste made of finely ground blanched almonds and sugar.

Bread crumbs or cubes, soft . . . Pieces or cubes that are torn or cut from fresh or day-old bread.

Brown sugar, granulated . . . Brown sugar processed to make granular. If used in recipes, follow label for substitution amounts.

Shortening . . . A hydrogenized fat made from vegetable or vegetable and animal fats. In a solid, yet pliable state.

Cooking oil . . . Fat in a liquid state.

Cream, whipping . . . Heavy cream that will become thick when whipped (about 30% butterfat).

Cream, light . . . Cream used in cooking but not high enough in butterfat to whip (about 20% butterfat).

Half and half . . . Very light cream — half milk, half cream.

Dairy sour cream . . . Cream that has been made sour by use of cultures. Do not substitute sour half and half or imitation sour cream in baking since the fat level, which is important as shortening, is lower.

Yogurt . . . Milk that has been soured by use of cultures.

Condensed milk (sweetened) . . . Canned whole milk from which the water has been evaporated and sugar has been added.

Evaporated milk . . . Canned whole milk from which half the water has been evaporated.

Prepared dried peel . . . Commercially prepared dried lemon or orange peel.

Pumpkin pie mix . . . A mixture of pumpkin, sugar and spices, of which there are two types available. One type has the liquid added so you just add eggs; the other needs both the eggs and liquid added. Check weights and directions carefully.

Measures

3 teaspoons	=	I tablespoon
I6 tablespoons	=	I cup
2 cups	=	I pint
2 pints	=	I quart
4 quarts	=	I gallon
8 fl. oz.	=	I cup
I6 oz.	=	I lb.

Can Sizes

Food	Quantity	Yields
Almonds	4 oz.	I cup diced roasted or I cup slivered
Apples	I medium	I cup chopped or I cup sliced
Blueberries	I lb. or I pint	2 cups fresh or frozen
Candied fruit	8 oz.	I½ cups, cut up
Candied peel	8 oz.	I½ cups
Cookies, creme-filled	I0 cookies	I cup crumbs
Crackers, graham	I5 crackers	I cup crumbs
Crackers, soda	20 crackers	I cup crumbs
Cream, whipping	I cup	2 cups whipped
Dates	I lb. (I6 oz.)	2 cups, cut up
Lemon	I lemon	2 to 3 teaspoons grated peel; 2 to 3 tablespoons juice
Milk, evaporated	6 oz. can I4½ oz. can	¾ cup I⅔ cup
Milk, sweetened condensed	I5½ oz. can	I⅓ cups
Orange	I medium	I to 2 tablespoons grated peel; ¼ to ⅓ cup juice
Peanuts	5 oz.	I cup
Pecans	4¼ oz. 3¾ oz.	I cup chopped I cup halves
Prunes	I lb.	3 cups, cut-up cooked
Sugar	I lb.	2 cups
Sugar, brown	I lb.	2¼ cups firmly packed
Sugar, confectioners'	I lb.	3½ cups
Walnuts	4½ oz. 3½ oz.	I cup chopped I cup halves

Substitutions

Apple pie spice . . . ½ teaspoon cinnamon, ¼ teaspoon nutmeg, ⅛ teaspoon allspice, ⅛ teaspoon cardamom = I teaspoon apple pie spice.

Buttermilk . . . I tablespoon vinegar plus milk to make I cup = I cup buttermilk or sour milk.

Chocolate . . . I envelope pre-melted unsweetened chocolate = I square unsweetened chocolate, melted.

Cornstarch . . . 2 tablespoons flour = I tablespoon cornstarch.

Lemon peel . . . I teaspoon prepared dried lemon peel = I teaspoon fresh grated lemon peel.

Orange peel . . . I teaspoon prepared dried orange peel = I teaspoon fresh grated orange peel.

Pumpkin pie spice . . . ½ teaspoon cinnamon, ¼ teaspoon ginger, ⅛ teaspoon allspice, ⅛ teaspoon nutmeg = I teaspoon pumpkin pie spice.

Quick-cooking tapioca . . . I tablespoon flour =2 teaspoons quick-cooking tapioca.

Equivalents

Size	Weight	Approximate Cups
4 oz.	4 oz.	½ cup
8 oz.	8 oz.	I cup
Picnic	10½ to 12 oz.	1¼ cups
12 oz. vacuum	12 oz.	1½ cups
#300	14 to 16 oz.	1¾ cups
#303	16 to 17 oz.	2 cups
#2	I lb. 4 oz. or I pt. 2 fl. oz.	2½ cups
#2½	I lb. 13 oz.	3½ cups
#3	3 lb. 3 oz. or I qt. 14 fl. oz.	5¾ cups
#10	6 lb. 8 oz. to 7 lb. 5 oz.	12 to 13 cups

Sauces &Toppings

• The finishing touch to most any dessert is the shiny sauce that embraces it, or the perky topping that gives it a special shape and flavor. A dessert that is fresh-from-the-oven one day can be reheated and come back with a new look and new taste under a distinctive sauce. Keep in mind that ready-to-eat ice cream toppings and other dessert sauces are easy put-ons. Remember that fresh or thawed frozen fruits are a spectacular finishing touch to ice cream and many other desserts. Your blender is a natural for sauce, and the manufacturer's instruction booklet is full of saucy ideas. Check them out.

Whipped cream, the topping terrific, can be bought as fresh "whipping cream" in the dairy section, or perhaps you prefer the already whipped and frozen topping. Don't forget the whipped topping mix (handily kept on your cupboard shelf) or the can of dairy topping in your refrigerator, that is so prettily dispensed from an aerosol can.

Here are some of the favorite sauces and toppings for dressing up your desserts.

Whipped Cream

I cup whipping cream
2 to 4 tablespoons sugar
½ teaspoon vanilla, if desired

2 CUPS TOPPING

Beat cream until slightly thickened. Blend in sugar and vanilla; beat until thickened.

Tip: *If desired, I to 2 tablespoons brandy, rum of favorite liqueur may be used for vanilla.*

Chocolate Whipped Cream

(Try on chocolate, vanilla, date or coffee flavored cakes and desserts.)

Add 2 tablespoons cocoa and dash of salt to whipping cream before beating. Use 4 tablespoons sugar.

Lemon Whipped Cream

Fold in 2 tablespoons lemonade concentrate along with sugar; omit vanilla.

Spicy Whipped Cream

(Delicious atop spicy brown sugar or date cakes and desserts.)

Add ⅛ teaspoon nutmeg and ⅛ teaspoon cinnamon along with sugar and vanilla.

Strawberry Cream Topping

(Delicious with vanilla, pineapple, lemon and cream cheese flavors.)

Fold ½ cup strawberry preserves or sweetened, sliced strawberries into whipped cream; omit sugar and vanilla.

Chocolate Sauce

    2 envelopes (2 ounces) pre-melted
       chocolate
    ¾ cup light corn syrup
    ½ cup water
    ⅛ teaspoon salt
    1 teaspoon vanilla

                              1½ CUPS SAUCE

Combine all ingredients except vanilla in medium saucepan. Cook over medium heat, stirring occasionally, until mixture boils. Boil gently 5 to 8 minutes. Blend in vanilla. Cool. Serve warm or cold. Store leftover in covered container in refrigerator.

Lemon Sauce

    ½ cup sugar
    2 tablespoons cornstarch
       Dash salt
    1 cup hot water
    2 teaspoons grated lemon peel
    2 tablespoons lemon juice
    2 tablespoons butter or margarine

                              1½ CUPS SAUCE

Combine sugar, cornstarch and salt in medium saucepan. Blend in water. Cook over medium heat, stirring constantly until mixture boils and is clear and slightly thickened. Stir in lemon peel, juice and butter. Serve warm or cold.

Easy Lemon, Chocolate, Vanilla, or Butterscotch Sauce

Prepare packaged pudding and pie filling mix as directed on package, adding ¼ cup additional liquid.

Easy Fruit Sauce

Thin canned fruit pie filling with water or fruit juice until of desired consistency.

Cooked Rhubarb Sauce

    4 cups (about 1 lb.) cut-up rhubarb
       (1-inch pieces)
    ¼ cup water
    ¾ cup sugar

                              2½ CUPS SAUCE

Place rhubarb and water in saucepan. Cover. Bring to boil. Boil gently over low heat, stirring occasionally until tender, about 20 minutes. Stir in sugar.

Cooked Applesauce

(Delicious warm or cold over cakes and desserts — especially gingerbread, spice and date flavors.)

    4 medium apples, peeled, cored and
       cut in eighths
    ½ cup water
    ¼ cup sugar

                              2½ CUPS SAUCE

Place apples and water in medium saucepan. Cover. Bring to boil. Boil gently over low heat, stirring occasionally until tender, about 20 to 25 minutes. Sieve or puree in blender, if desired. Stir in sugar. Cook until sugar is dissolved. If desired, add ½ teaspoon cinnamon or ½ teaspoon nutmeg.

Uncooked Applesauce

(Serve immediately as it browns on standing. Deliciously different over warm gingerbread, spice or date cakes.)

    ¼ cup liquid (water or fruit juice)
    2 tablespoons lemon juice
    4 apples, cored and cut in eighths
    ¼ cup sugar
    ⅛ teaspoon cinnamon

                              2¼ CUPS SAUCE

Place liquid and lemon juice and 4 or 5 pieces of apple in blender container. Cover and process at "puree" or low speed until smooth. Increase speed to "blend" or medium. Remove feeder cap and add remaining apples a few at a time, processing until smooth. Add sugar and cinnamon.

Tip: In late winter, apples are less juicy. You may need to add 1 to 2 tablespoons more liquid.

Toppings at a Glance

You can mix and switch dessert sauces and toppings as easily as you can change an outfit with a new hat. Special sauces and toppings are given for many of the bake off recipes in this book. Here's how you can locate a favorite one easily, and other suggestions for using it.

Name of Sauce or Topping	Page Number
Apple Fluff Topping	Ginger Cake Apple Fluff 25
Caramel Cream Topping	Banana Caramel Cream Pie 98
Cinnamon Whipped Cream	Quick Banana Buns 40
Coffee Filling	Date Cream Roll 118
Egg Nog Topping	Pumpkin-Nog Pie 84
Orange Whipped Cream Topping	Orange Cheese Pie 96
Pink Frozen Cream Topping	Ruby Razz Crunch 43
Sour Cream Topping	Cherry Honeys 136
Whipped Cream Topping	Graham Cracker Nut Dessert 30
Whipped Cheese Topping	Magnolia Manor Dessert 25
Hard Sauce	Orange Festival Pudding 49
Butter Sauce	Sugarplum Cake 50
Butterscotch Sauce	New England Fruit Pudding 55
Caramel Sauce	Walnut Sundae Torte 55
Milk Sauce	Grandmother's Dessert Rolls 32
Nutmeg Sauce	My Mother's Pudding 48
Orange Sauce	Magnolia Manor Dessert 25

What it is	Be creative; try it on —
Whipped cream with applesauce.	Use as topping spooned over gingerbread, spicy cakes, date or nut tortes or cakes.
Brown sugar whipped cream.	Perfect complement for date, coffee, spice, peach and chocolate flavors.
Whipped cream with cinnamon and sugar.	Serve over squares of spicy cake and gingerbread.
Coffee whipped cream.	Perfect with date, chocolate, spice or nut cakes and desserts.
Whipped topping with egg nog added.	Serve at holiday time over pumpkin or mince pie or over steamed pudding.
Orange whipped cream.	Serve atop orange cake, gingerbread, spice or chocolate cakes.
Whipped cream and raspberries frozen in fluffy mounds.	Dress up any cake or bar that is served warm. Place on just before serving. Try mounds atop wedges of warm peach pie.
Whipped cream and sour cream; add coconut if desired.	Use as whipped cream or ice cream where you want a special tartness.
Whipped cream made flavorful and stable with dry frosting mix.	Use like you would whipped cream, or try as frosting on your next shortening or angel food cake. Try different flavors of frosting — refrigerate cakes several hours to mellow flavors before serving.
Cream cheese whipped fluffy and smooth, sweetened and flavored.	Use like you would whipped cream. Especially good on spicy cakes or as pleasant topper for dishes of fruit.
Like what's served at Christmas time — butter, sugar and a hint of rum or brandy.	Serve over something warm and spicy.
Interesting blend of brown sugar and buttermilk.	Pour over steamed pudding or spice, date, prune, apple or banana cakes.
Like the kind you serve over ice cream.	Pour over steamed pudding, spice and other heavy, moist cakes or ice cream.
Like caramel ice cream sauce.	Spoon over nut, spice or fruit cakes, ice cream, baked apples, or steamed puddings.
Thickened milk-butter sauce.	Pour over baked fruits, crisps or cobblers. Excellent over apple and spicy desserts.
Thickened butter-type sauce that's served warm.	Serve over anything spicy or that goes with spice — apple, date, peach, banana, etc. flavors.
Thickened tangy orange sauce served warm or cold.	Spoon a little over cheesecake, or just drizzle over the whipped cream that tops your favorite pudding. Try over pancakes and waffles, too.

Desserts
Warm From
The Oven

● The spicy aroma of an oven dessert puts a certain amount of anticipation in the air that makes your whole meal more enjoyable.

These are the "serve me warm" recipes: pudding cakes (with the sauce baked under the cake), gingerbreads, apple dumplings, cobblers and cakes that are best while still warm — they all speak of warmth and home and happy eating. Some can be made ahead and reheated. Light the hearth and have an aromatic oven dessert tonight.

As pretty a cobbler as you've ever passed your plate for. Sweet crumb topping garnishes the biscuit topping, and you can top it all off with cream in just over an hour, if you wish.

Peach Easy Dessert

    I can (I lb. I3 oz.) or 2 cups peach
      slices, drained
    ¼ cup sugar
    ½ teaspoon cinnamon

Biscuit Topping
    I cup Pillsbury's Best All Purpose Flour*
    3 tablespoons sugar
    2 teaspoons baking powder
    ½ teaspoon salt
    ¼ cup milk
    2 tablespoons cooking oil
    I egg

Crumb Topping
    2 tablespoons sugar
    I tablespoon flour
    2 tablespoons butter or margarine

OVEN 400°   8 SERVINGS

Place peach slices in bottom of 8-inch square pan which has been greased on bottom only. Sprinkle with sugar and cinnamon. Drop Biscuit Topping by spoonfuls onto the peaches. Sprinkle with Crumb Topping. Bake at 400° for 30 to 35 minutes until golden brown and bubbly. Serve warm with cream, if desired.

Biscuit Topping: In small mixing bowl, combine flour, sugar, baking powder and salt. Combine milk, oil and egg; add to dry ingredients all at once. Stir until all dry ingredients are moistened.

Crumb Topping: Combine sugar, flour and butter until mixture resembles coarse crumbs.

*For use with Pillsbury's Best Self-Rising Flour, omit baking powder and salt.

Canned pears and gingerale bubble beneath a topping of refrigerated caramel rolls. Quickly done in less than an hour.

Perky Pear Cobbler

    I can (I lb. I3 oz.) pear halves, drain
      and reserve I cup syrup
    ¼ cup Pillsbury's Best All Purpose Flour*
    ½ teaspoon grated lemon peel
    ¼ teaspoon salt
    Dash of ginger
    I cup gingerale
    I tablespoon butter or margarine
    I can Pillsbury Refrigerated Quick
      Caramel Rolls with Nuts

OVEN 400°   8 SERVINGS

Cube pears and place in 2-quart casserole. In saucepan, combine flour, lemon peel, salt, ginger, gingerale, reserved syrup and sugar-nut mixture from can of caramel rolls; mix well. Cook, over medium heat, stirring occasionally, until thick; stir in butter. Pour over pears. Separate caramel rolls; arrange on top of sauce. Bake at 400° for 25 to 30 minutes until golden brown. Serve warm.

*For use with Pillsbury's Best Self-Rising Flour, omit salt.

Bright red cherry-rhubarb filling peeks out between ready-made refrigerated biscuits. Serve warm in an hour.

Hidden Glory Cobbler

    I can (I lb. 5 oz.) prepared cherry pie
      filling
    I package (I lb.) frozen rhubarb, thawed
    I can (8 oz.) Pillsbury Refrigerated Flaky
      Tenderflake Baking Powder Biscuits
    Melted butter
    Sugar

OVEN 425°   6 TO 8 SERVINGS

In saucepan, combine cherry filling and rhubarb; heat until mixture begins to bubble. Separate biscuits; press 9 onto bottom of 9-inch square pan (reserve remaining biscuits for top of cobbler). Pour hot fruit filling over crust. Peel each of the remaining biscuits apart to make 3 thin biscuits. Place on top of fruit filling; brush with butter and sprinkle with sugar. Bake at 425° for 20 to 25 minutes until golden brown and bubbly. Serve warm with whipped cream.

A cobbler never cobbled as quickly as this recipe goes together, because you have a head start with prepared ingredients. Cinnamoney rolls on a colorful cherry pie filling.

Cherry Cinnamon Cobbler

 1 can (1 lb. 5 oz.) prepared cherry pie
    filling
 1 can Pillsbury Refrigerated Quick
    Cinnamon Rolls with Icing
 2 tablespoons butter or margarine, melted
 ¼ cup chopped pecans
 ⅛ teaspoon grated lemon peel

OVEN 400°   6 TO 8 SERVINGS

Pour pie filling into an 8-inch round layer pan. Heat at 400° for 15 minutes. Separate cinnamon rolls and dip edges in butter, then in pecans. Arrange, topping side up, on top of hot pie filling. Bake at 400° for 25 to 30 minutes until golden brown. Combine lemon peel and icing; spread on rolls.

Tip: Other favorite prepared pie fillings, such as apple or peach, may be substituted for the cherry.

Golden peaches and red raspberries from the freezer with a hint of ginger make for a pleasant surprise under a tender cakey cobbler topping.

Peach Melba Special

Filling

¼ cup sugar

1½ tablespoons cornstarch

1 teaspoon finely chopped preserved or ground ginger

¼ cup butter or margarine

1 package (10 oz.) frozen peaches, drain and reserve syrup

1 package (10 oz.) frozen red raspberries, drain and reserve syrup

Sugar

Topping

1 cup Pillsbury's Best All Purpose Flour*

¼ cup sugar

2 teaspoons baking powder

½ teaspoon salt

¼ cup butter or margarine

¼ cup shortening

⅓ cup water

OVEN 375°　　　　　5 TO 6 SERVINGS

Filling: In saucepan, combine sugar, cornstarch, ginger, butter and reserved syrups. Cook over medium heat, stirring occasionally, until thickened. Stir in fruit; pour into 8-inch round baking dish. Drop spoonfuls of Topping onto fruit mixture. Sprinkle with sugar. Bake at 375° for 35 to 40 minutes until golden brown. Serve warm, plain or with ice cream.

Topping: In mixing bowl, combine flour, sugar, baking powder and salt. Cut in butter and shortening until particles are fine. Add water; stir just until blended.

*For use with Pillsbury's Best Self-Rising Flour, omit baking powder and salt.

Comes from the oven sugar-crusted with bubbling peach and blueberry filling underneath the cobbler topping. One hour and fifteen minutes.

Peach-Berry Cobbler

1 can (1 lb. 5 oz.) prepared peach pie filling

1 cup blueberries, fresh or frozen

1 tablespoon lemon juice

2 tablespoons sugar

¼ teaspoon nutmeg

Cobbler Topping

1 cup Pillsbury's Best All Purpose Flour*

½ cup sugar

1½ teaspoons baking powder

½ teaspoon salt

½ cup milk

¼ cup butter or margarine, softened

OVEN 375°　　　　　6 TO 8 SERVINGS

In 2-quart baking dish, combine peach filling, blueberries and lemon juice. Heat at 375° for 15 minutes. Spoon Cobbler Topping over warm fruit. Sprinkle with sugar and nutmeg. Bake at 375° for 40 to 45 minutes until golden brown and bubbly. Serve warm.

Cobbler Topping: In small mixing bowl, combine flour, sugar, baking powder and salt. Add milk and butter; beat until smooth.

*For use with Pillsbury's Best Self-Rising Flour, omit baking powder and salt.

Blushing Beauty Dumplings

    I can Pillsbury Refrigerated Quick Crescent Dinner Rolls
    4 medium baking apples, peeled and cored
    4 tablespoons orange marmalade
    Nutmeg
    4 teaspoons butter or margarine
    ¼ cup light corn syrup
    5 drops red food coloring

OVEN 350°   4 DUMPLINGS

Unroll crescent dough. Separate into 4 rectangles. Press to seal perforations of each rectangle. Wrap a rectangle of dough around sides of each apple, sealing bottom and sides and bringing top just to edges of cavity; pinch edges well to seal. Place at least one inch apart in 8 or 9-inch square pan. Spoon I tablespoon orange marmalade into cavity of each apple; sprinkle with nutmeg and top each with I teaspoon butter. Bake at 350° for 50 to 55 minutes or until apples are tender. Combine corn syrup and food coloring; spoon over tops of dumplings allowing to drizzle down sides. Serve warm, plain or with cream.

Fruit flavors mingle for a new taste tingle in these apple-meets-apricot dumplings. Note the time-saving tip for an easy turnover variation.

Applecots

    2 cups Pillsbury's Best All Purpose Flour*
    2 teaspoons baking powder
    I teaspoon salt
    ⅔ cup shortening
    ½ cup milk
    I can (I lb.) apricot halves, drain and reserve syrup
    3 apples, peeled, cored and cut in half

<u>Syrup</u>
    I½ cups liquid (apricot syrup plus water)
    ⅓ cup sugar
    2 tablespoons butter or margarine
    ¼ teaspoon cinnamon

OVEN 375°   6 DUMPLINGS

In large mixing bowl, combine flour, baking powder and salt. Cut in shortening until particles are the size of small peas. Add milk; stir until dough forms a ball. Roll out on floured surface to an 18x12-inch rectangle. Cut into six 6-inch squares. Place 2 apricot halves on each square; top each with apple half, cut-side down. Bring opposite corners to center and pinch together sealing edges. Place in ungreased 13x9-inch pan. Pour hot Syrup over dumplings. Bake at 375° for 50 to 55 minutes or until apples are tender. Spoon sauce over dumplings to glaze. Serve warm with cream.

<u>Syrup</u>: Combine all ingredients in saucepan. Bring to boil.

<u>Tip</u>: For Applecot Turnovers, prepare I package Pillsbury Refrigerated Apple Turnover Pastries as directed on package, placing I apricot half on top of apple filling in each turnover. Seal edges only at point. Bake as directed.

*For use with Pillsbury's Best Self-Rising Flour, omit baking powder and salt.

Dainty apple wrap-ups crusty-baked in a juicy sauce and served warm. Crescent dough makes them super quick and easy in less than an hour.

Spicy Apple Twists

    2 large apples, peeled and cored
    I can Pillsbury Refrigerated Quick Crescent Dinner Rolls
    2 tablespoons butter or margarine, melted
    ½ cup sugar
    I teaspoon cinnamon
    ¼ cup orange juice or water

OVEN 400°   4 TO 6 SERVINGS

Cut each apple into eight pieces. Unroll crescent roll dough; separate into 8 triangles. Cut each in half lengthwise to make 16 triangle strips. Place an apple piece at wide end of each strip; roll up. Arrange in 9-inch square pan. Drizzle with butter; sprinkle with mixture of sugar and cinnamon. Pour orange juice or water into pan, but not over dumplings. Bake at 400° for 30 to 35 minutes or until apples are tender. Serve warm, plain or with cream.

Spicy Apple Twists

An upside-down cake with pears like flower petals set with caramel on a spice cake. For a real fiesta, bring it in flaming, in an hour and fifteen minutes.

Spicy Pear Fiesta

Pear Topping

    ¼ cup butter or margarine
    ⅔ cup firmly packed brown sugar
    I tablespoon flour
    I tablespoon water or pear syrup
    I can (I lb.) pear halves, drained

Spice Cake

    1½ cups Pillsbury's Best All Purpose Flour*
    ¾ cup firmly packed brown sugar
    ¼ cup sugar
    2 teaspoons baking powder
    I teaspoon cinnamon
    ½ teaspoon salt
    ¼ teaspoon cloves
    ⅔ cup milk
    ⅓ cup shortening
    I egg

OVEN 350°   6 TO 8 SERVINGS

Pear Topping: Melt butter in 9-inch round layer pan or 9-inch square pan in oven. Stir in brown sugar, flour and water. Place pear halves cut-side down in brown sugar mixture, tips pointing toward the center. Do not place pear in center. Pour Spice Cake batter over pears, spreading to cover. Bake at 350° for 45 to 55 minutes until top springs back when touched lightly in center. Cool 2 minutes, loosen edges with spatula; invert onto serving plate. Serve warm.

Spice Cake: In large mixer bowl, combine all ingredients at lowest speed until well blended.

Tip: For flaming dessert, soak sugar cubes in lemon extract before serving. Place a cube in each pear; ignite.

*For use with Pillsbury's Best Self-Rising Flour, omit baking powder and salt.

HIGH ALTITUDE ADJUSTMENT — 5,200 FEET. Reduce baking powder to I teaspoon.

So good you'll need seconds for everyone. A one-step apple cake with caramel pudding sauce underneath—crunchy with chopped almonds. An hour and a half does it.

Caramel Apple Pudding

¾ cup Pillsbury's Best All Purpose Flour*
½ cup sugar
  1 teaspoon baking powder
  1 teaspoon cinnamon
¼ teaspoon salt
½ cup milk
1½ cups coarsely chopped apples
½ cup chopped almonds

Sauce
¾ cup firmly packed brown sugar
¼ cup butter or margarine
¾ cup boiling water

OVEN 375°   6 SERVINGS

In mixing bowl, combine flour, sugar, baking powder, cinnamon, salt, milk, apples and almonds; blend thoroughly. Spread in greased 1½ quart casserole. Pour Sauce over batter. Bake at 375° for 40 to 50 minutes until golden brown. Serve warm with ice cream or whipped cream.

Sauce: Combine brown sugar, butter and water; stir until butter is melted.

Tip: 8-inch square pan, which has been greased on bottom only, may be used.

*For use with Pillsbury's Best Self-Rising Flour, omit baking powder and salt.

Under a pink and pretty strawberry whipped cream topping are squares of an easy-to-make pineapple-strawberry upside down cake. Ready in an hour.

Strawberry Sunshine Dessert

  1 tablespoon butter or margarine
  1 can (1 lb. 4½ oz.) crushed pineapple, drained
½ cup strawberry preserves
⅓ cup firmly packed brown sugar
  1 tablespoon flour
  1 package Pillsbury One Layer White Batter Cake Mix

OVEN 350°   9 SERVINGS

Melt butter in 8-inch square pan in oven. Add pineapple and preserves; spread evenly in bottom of pan. Combine brown sugar and flour; sprinkle over mixture.

Prepare cake mix as directed on package. Pour batter over pineapple mixture. Bake at 350° for 35 to 40 minutes until top springs back when touched lightly in center. Cool 2 minutes; loosen edges with spatula; invert onto serving plate. Serve warm with Strawberry Cream Topping, page 10.

Tips: Sliced, sweetened fresh strawberries may be used in place of strawberry preserves.

Use a Pillsbury Two-Layer White Batter Cake Mix. Prepare as directed on package. Use half of batter for this dessert, bake a layer from other half and freeze for later use.

HIGH ALTITUDE ADJUSTMENT—Follow cake mix package recommendations.

Dates and raisins in the cake, the zing of lemon peel in the caramel sauce. This is a one-step pudding-cake. One hour plus.

Family Caramel Pudding

Cake
  1 cup Pillsbury's Best All Purpose Flour*
½ cup sugar
1½ teaspoons baking powder
½ teaspoon salt
½ cup milk
  2 tablespoons cooking oil or melted butter
¼ cup raisins
¼ cup chopped dates

Caramel Sauce
1¼ cups water
⅔ cup firmly packed brown sugar
  2 tablespoons butter or margarine
  1 teaspoon grated lemon peel

OVEN 350°   6 TO 8 SERVINGS

Cake: In mixing bowl, combine flour, sugar, baking powder, salt, milk and oil; beat until well blended. Fold in raisins and dates. Spread in 8-inch square pan which has been greased on the bottom only. Pour Caramel Sauce over Cake. Bake at 350° for 40 to 45 minutes. Serve warm with whipped cream.

Caramel Sauce: Combine water, brown sugar and butter in saucepan. Bring to boil; boil gently 5 minutes. Add lemon peel.

*For use with Pillsbury's Best Self-Rising Flour, omit baking powder and salt.

Pecan-sprinkled gingerbread puts on a sweet Southern accent with cream cheese topping and orange sauce. Y'all come have a warm square of it in forty minutes.

Magnolia Manor Dessert

Gingerbread

    I package Pillsbury Gingerbread Mix

    ½ cup chopped pecans

Whipped Cheese Topping

    I package (8 oz.) cream cheese, softened

    ½ cup confectioners' sugar

    2 tablespoons light cream

    I teaspoon vanilla

Orange Sauce

    ½ cup sugar

    2 tablespoons cornstarch

    ⅛ teaspoon salt

    I cup orange juice

    2 tablespoons butter or margarine

    2 tablespoons lemon juice

    I tablespoon grated orange peel

OVEN 375°   8 TO 10 SERVINGS

Gingerbread: Prepare gingerbread mix as directed on package. Pour into 9-inch square pan which has been greased on the bottom only. Sprinkle with pecans. Bake at 375° for 25 to 30 minutes until cake springs back when touched lightly in center. Serve warm, cut in squares, topped with Whipped Cheese Topping and warm Orange Sauce.

Whipped Cheese Topping: Combine cream cheese, confectioners' sugar, cream and vanilla; beat until light and fluffy.

Orange Sauce: Combine sugar, cornstarch and salt in medium saucepan. Stir in orange juice and butter. Cook over medium heat, stirring constantly until clear and thickened. Remove from heat; stir in lemon juice and orange peel.

HIGH ALTITUDE ADJUSTMENT — Follow gingerbread mix package recommendations.

The topping takes the cake . . . as clever and chilly a combination as ever graced a gingerbread. Made with a mix in 45 minutes! See page 12 for other ways to use the topping.

Ginger Cake Apple Fluff

Gingerbread

    I package Pillsbury Gingerbread Mix

    ¼ cup chopped nuts

    2 tablespoons sugar

    ¼ teaspoon cinnamon

Apple Fluff

    I cup whipping cream

    I cup applesauce

    ½ cup confectioners' sugar

    2 tablespoons lemon juice

OVEN 375°   8 TO 10 SERVINGS

Gingerbread: Prepare gingerbread as directed on package. Pour into 8 or 9-inch square pan which has been greased on the bottom only. Combine nuts, sugar and cinnamon; sprinkle over batter. Bake at 375° for 30 to 35 minutes until cake springs back when touched lightly in center. Serve warm, cut in squares, topped with Apple Fluff.

Apple Fluff: Beat cream until thickened. Fold in applesauce, confectioners' sugar and lemon juice. Chill thoroughly.

Tips: Apple Fluff will keep several days, covered, in refrigerator.

To reheat gingerbread, wrap in foil; place in 350° oven for 10 to 15 minutes.

HIGH ALTITUDE ADJUSTMENT — Follow gingerbread mix package recommendations.

Great for George's birthday . . . or anybody's. Tart sour cherry upside down cake colorfully climaxed with a pretty red cherry sauce. Serve warm in sixty minutes.

Mount Vernon Dessert

Cherry Filling
> I can (I lb.) sour pie cherries, drain and
>   reserve juice
> 2 tablespoons butter or margarine,
>   softened
> ⅓ cup firmly packed brown sugar

Cake
> 1¾ cups Pillsbury's Best All Purpose Flour*
> I cup sugar
> 2 teaspoons baking powder
> ½ teaspoon salt
> ⅓ cup shortening
> ¾ cup milk
> I teaspoon vanilla
> I egg

Cherry Sauce
> 1½ cups liquid (juice from cherries
>   plus water)
> ½ cup sugar
> 2 tablespoons cornstarch
> ⅛ teaspoon almond extract
> ⅛ teaspoon red food coloring

OVEN 350°   9 SERVINGS

Cherry Filling: In 9-inch square pan, combine cherries, butter and brown sugar. Pour Cake batter over mixture. Bake at 350° for 35 to 45 minutes until top springs back when touched lightly. Cool 5 minutes; invert onto serving plate. Serve warm with Cherry Sauce.

Cake: In large mixer bowl, combine all ingredients at lowest speed; beat 2 minutes at medium speed.

Cherry Sauce: In medium saucepan, combine liquid, sugar and cornstarch. Cook over medium heat, stirring constantly, until thickened. Remove from heat. Add almond extract and food coloring.

*For use with Pillsbury's Best Self-Rising Flour, omit baking powder and salt.

HIGH ALTITUDE ADJUSTMENT — 5,200 FEET. Reduce baking powder to 1½ teaspoons.

Cherry-filled apples peek through golden dough wrappers in this recipe made super-easy with refrigerated turnover dough. Easy way to apples baked in a crust.

Apple Orchard Snowballs

> I package Pillsbury Refrigerated Quick
>   Cherry Turnover Pastries
> 4 medium baking apples, peeled and cored
>   Milk

Topping
> I cup whipping cream
>   Remainder of turnover filling

OVEN 350°   4 DUMPLINGS

Unroll turnover dough. Form into 4 rectangles by pinching together two pieces of dough at perforations. Wrap pieces of dough around sides of apples, sealing side well and letting dough extend I inch above top and bottom. Bring bottom edges together and seal well. Fill apple cavities with turnover filling, saving remainder for Topping. Bring top edges of dough together and seal well. Place on ungreased cookie sheet. Brush dough with milk. Bake at 350° for 50 to 55 minutes or until apples are tender. Drizzle tops with turnover glaze. Serve warm with topping.

Topping: Beat cream until thickened. Fold in remainder of turnover filling.

Tip: For variety, try Pillsbury Refrigerated Apple or Blueberry Turnover Pastries.

Pears and mincemeat make beautiful music together in this autumn treat. Appetites come alive while it's baking in the oven. Serve it in an hour and a half.

Mincey Pear Cobbler

Filling
>   3 medium pears, peeled and sliced
> ¼ cup Pillsbury's Best All Purpose or
>   Self-Rising Flour*
> ¼ cup firmly packed brown sugar
> ½ cup prepared mincemeat
>   1 tablespoon lemon juice
>   4 tablespoons butter, melted

Topping
>   1 cup Pillsbury's Best All Purpose Flour*
> 1½ teaspoons baking powder
> ½ teaspoon salt
>   1 egg
>   Milk
>   2 tablespoons oil or melted butter
> ⅓ cup prepared mincemeat

Crunchy Topping
> ¼ cup sugar
> ¼ cup finely chopped walnuts
> ¼ teaspoon cinnamon

OVEN 375°   6 TO 8 SERVINGS

Filling: Arrange pears on bottom of 8-inch square pan; sprinkle with flour and brown sugar. Combine mincemeat and lemon juice; spoon over pears. Drizzle with 3 tablespoons butter. Drop Topping by tablespoonfuls onto fruit mixture. Sprinkle with Crunchy Topping; drizzle with remaining tablespoon butter. Bake at 375° for 30 to 35 minutes until golden brown. Serve warm with whipped cream, if desired.

Topping: Combine flour, baking powder and salt in mixing bowl. Mix egg with enough milk to make ⅓ cup; stir in oil and mincemeat. Add all at once to dry ingredients; stir until dough clings together.

Crunchy Topping: Combine all ingredients in small bowl.

Tip: 1 can (1 lb. 14 oz.) pears, drained and sliced, may be substituted for fresh pears. Decrease brown sugar to 2 tablespoons.

*For use with Pillsbury's Best Self-Rising Flour, omit baking powder and salt.

A flavor combination worth talking about . . . juicy apple crisp with a peanut butter crumb topping. Big hit with the youngsters.

Apple Peanut Spoon Dessert

>   4 cups (4 medium) peeled, sliced apples
> ½ cup sugar
>   1 tablespoon flour
> ½ teaspoon cinnamon
> ¼ teaspoon nutmeg
>   2 tablespoons lemon juice

Topping
> ¾ cup Pillsbury's Best All Purpose Flour*
> ⅓ cup sugar
> ¼ teaspoon soda
> ¼ teaspoon salt
> ¼ cup shortening
> ¼ cup milk
>   2 tablespoons peanut butter
>   1 egg

OVEN 350°   6 TO 8 SERVINGS

In 9-inch pie pan or 1½-quart casserole, combine apples, sugar, flour, cinnamon, nutmeg and lemon juice. Drop Topping by spoonfuls over apple mixture and spread carefully. Bake at 350° for 35 to 40 minutes until golden brown and apples are tender. Spoon into serving dishes and serve warm with whipped cream.

Topping: In large mixer bowl, combine all ingredients at lowest speed until dry ingredients are moistened. Beat at high speed 2 minutes.

Tip: 1 can prepared apple pie filling may be used for apple filling.

*For use with Pillsbury's Best Self-Rising Flour, omit soda and salt.

Delicious orange dumplings, enhanced with coconut, bake atop an orangey sauce. Make it extra quick with the refrigerated roll tip.

Orange Pudding Dumplings

> I cup sugar
> 3 tablespoons cornstarch
> I tablespoon flour
> I cup water
> I cup orange juice
> ¼ cup lemon juice
> ½ cup flaked coconut

Orange Dumplings

> I½ cups Pillsbury's Best All Purpose Flour*
> ⅔ cup sugar
> I tablespoon baking powder
> ½ teaspoon salt
> ¼ cup shortening
> ⅔ cup orange juice

OVEN 350°   8 TO 10 SERVINGS

Combine all ingredients in saucepan. Cook over medium heat, stirring occasionally, until mixture thickens. Pour into 8-inch square pan. Drop Orange Dumplings by heaping tablespoons into sauce. Sprinkle with coconut. Bake at 350° for 35 to 40 minutes until golden brown. Serve warm with whipped cream.

Orange Dumplings: In mixing bowl, combine flour, sugar, baking powder and salt. Cut in shortening until particles are fine. Stir in orange juice until all dry ingredients are moistened.

Tips: Reconstituted frozen orange juice may be used for orange juice.

If desired, use I can Pillsbury Quick Orange Danish Rolls with Icing in place of Orange Dumplings, sprinkling rolls with ½ cup flaked coconut before baking. After baking, frost with Icing.

*For use with Pillsbury's Best Self-Rising Flour, omit baking powder and salt.

Serve this warm and aromatic: sweet fruit (could be pears, apricots, peaches or pineapple) in thickened sauce, topped with spicy crumb topping and clouds of meringue. Make and bake in an hour.

Heavenly Pears

Filling

> I can (I lb. 13 oz.) pear halves, drain and reserve I cup syrup
> 2 egg yolks
> ¼ cup sugar
> 2 tablespoons flour
> 2 tablespoons lemon juice

Topping

> ⅔ cup Pillsbury's Best All Purpose Flour*
> ⅔ cup graham cracker crumbs
> ½ cup chopped nuts
> ⅓ cup firmly packed brown sugar
> ¼ teaspoon salt
> ¼ teaspoon soda
> ½ teaspoon cinnamon
> ½ teaspoon vanilla
> ½ cup butter or margarine, melted

Meringue

> 2 egg whites
> ¼ cup sugar
> ½ teaspoon cinnamon

OVEN 375°   6 TO 8 SERVINGS

Filling: In saucepan, combine reserved pear syrup, egg yolks, sugar, flour and lemon juice. Cook over medium heat, stirring constantly, until mixture comes to a boil. Boil I minute. Pour into greased 2-quart casserole. Arrange pear halves over sauce. Sprinkle with Topping. Bake at 375° for 30 to 35 minutes until golden brown. Drop Meringue by spoonfuls around edge of hot casserole. Bake 5 minutes more.

Topping: In small mixing bowl, combine all Topping ingredients. Mix together until well blended.

Meringue: In small mixer bowl, beat egg whites at high speed until soft peaks are formed. Gradually add sugar and cinnamon; continue beating until stiff peaks form.

Tip: If desired, I can (I lb. 13 oz.) apricot halves, peach halves or pineapple rings may be substituted for pears.

*For use with Pillsbury's Best Self-Rising Flour, omit salt and soda in Topping.

Double Quick Date Dessert

    I cup Pillsbury's Best All Purpose Flour*
    ¾ cup sugar
    ½ teaspoon soda
    ¼ teaspoon salt
    ½ cup hot water
    2 tablespoons butter or margarine, softened
    ½ teaspoon vanilla
    I cup dates, cut in large pieces
    ¼ cup chopped walnuts

OVEN 350°   6 TO 8 SERVINGS

Combine all ingredients in large mixing bowl. Stir until all particles are moistened. Spread batter in greased and floured 8-inch square pan. Bake at 350° for 25 to 30 minutes until top springs back when touched lightly in center. Serve warm, cut in squares, with whipped cream or ice cream.

*With Pillsbury's Best Self-Rising Flour, omit salt.

HIGH ALTITUDE ADJUSTMENT — 5,200 FEET. Increase flour to 1¼ cups.

The ingenious use of watermelon pickles gives the warm and spicy cake an unusually good flavor. Under an hour to serving time.

County Fair Watermelon Dessert

    2 cups Pillsbury's Best All Purpose Flour*
    I cup firmly packed brown sugar
    I teaspoon soda
    I teaspoon salt
    2 teaspoons cinnamon
    ½ teaspoon nutmeg
    ½ cup shortening
    I cup dairy sour cream
    2 eggs
    I cup finely chopped watermelon pickles

OVEN 350°   13x9-INCH CAKE

In large mixer bowl, blend all ingredients, except watermelon pickles, at lowest speed. Beat I minute at medium speed. Stir in watermelon pickles. Spread batter evenly in greased and floured 13x9-inch pan. Bake at 350° for 30 to 35 minutes. Serve warm with Spicy Whipped Cream page 10.

*With Pillsbury's Best Self-Rising Flour, omit salt.

A rich and rummy whipped cream topping caps a cake textured with graham crackers, pecans and dates. Start an hour and a half before serving.

Graham Cracker Nut Dessert

    I cup Pillsbury's Best All Purpose Flour*
    ¾ cup firmly packed brown sugar
    2 teaspoons baking powder
    ½ teaspoon salt
    I cup milk
    ⅓ cup cooking oil
    I teaspoon rum flavoring
    2 eggs
    I cup graham cracker crumbs
    ½ cup chopped pecans
    ¾ cup dates, cut up
      Pecan halves, if desired

Whipped Cream Topping
    I package Pillsbury One Layer Size Vanilla
      Buttercream Frosting Mix
    I cup whipping cream
    ¼ teaspoon rum flavoring

OVEN 350°   8 TO 10 SERVINGS

In large mixer bowl, combine flour, brown sugar, baking powder, salt, milk, oil, rum flavoring and eggs at lowest speed. Beat 2 minutes at medium speed. Stir in graham cracker crumbs and pecans. Pour into 9-inch square pan which has been greased on the bottom only. Sprinkle with dates. Bake at 350° for 35 to 40 minutes until top springs back when touched lightly in center. Serve warm, cut in squares, with Whipped Cream Topping. Garnish each serving with pecan half.

Whipped Cream Topping: In small mixer bowl, combine dry frosting mix, whipping cream and rum flavoring; beat until thickened.

Tip: Half of a regular size package of frosting mix may be used for one layer size.

*For use with Pillsbury's Best Self-Rising Flour, omit baking powder and salt.

HIGH ALTITUDE ADJUSTMENT — 5,200 FEET. Reduce baking powder to I teaspoon.

Old Virginia Cobbler

>   2 cans (I lb. 5 oz. each) prepared apple
>   pie filling
> ½ teaspoon grated lemon peel
> ¼ teaspoon nutmeg
> ½ to I tablespoon lemon juice
>   I can Pillsbury Refrigerated Quick
>   Crescent Dinner Rolls
>   Milk
>   Sugar

OVEN 400°   8 SERVINGS

In greased 2-quart casserole, combine pie filling, lemon peel, nutmeg and lemon juice. Heat at 400° for 15 minutes. Unroll crescent dough and separate into 8 triangles. Place one triangle on top of hot filling, point at center; roll up excess of wide end until it fits casserole. Continue with remaining triangles just slightly overlapping points in center. Brush dough with milk and sprinkle with sugar. Bake at 400° for 20 to 25 minutes until gold brown. Serve warm, plain or with whipped cream.

Whole baked apples captured in cinnamon streusel coffee cake. Ready to serve warm — perhaps with whipped cream — in a little over an hour.

Baked Apple Puff

>   5 medium baking apples, peeled and cored
>   I package Pillsbury Cinnamon Streusel
>   Coffee Cake Mix
>   2 tablespoons raisins
>   2 tablespoons chopped nuts

OVEN 375°   5 LARGE SERVINGS

Coat apples with ¼ cup of topping from coffee cake mix. Place in 9-inch square pan which has been greased on the bottom only. Fill center of apples with raisins and ¼ cup more of topping. Prepare coffee cake mix as directed on package. Spread batter between apples. Sprinkle with remaining ½ cup of topping and the nuts. Bake at 375° for 30 to 35 minutes until cake springs back when touched lightly in center. Serve warm with plain or whipped cream.

HIGH ALTITUDE ADJUSTMENT — 5,200 FEET.
Add I tablespoon milk to batter, bake at 375° for 35 to 40 minutes.

Grandmother's Dessert Rolls

Dessert Rolls

>   2 cups Pillsbury's Best All Purpose Flour*
>   I tablespoon baking powder
>   I teaspoon salt
> ¾ cup milk
>   2 tablespoons cooking oil
> ½ cup sugar
>   I teaspoon cinnamon
> ⅓ cup butter or margarine

Milk Sauce

> ¼ cup sugar
>   3 tablespoons flour
> ¼ teaspoon salt
>   2 cups milk
>   2 tablespoons butter
>   I teaspoon vanilla

OVEN 400°   8 SERVINGS

Dessert Rolls: In mixing bowl, combine flour, baking powder, salt, milk and oil. Stir until dough clings together. Knead on floured surface 10 to 12 times. Roll out to a 16x8-inch rectangle. Cut into eight 4-inch squares.

Combine sugar and cinnamon. Cut in butter until mixture resembles coarse crumbs. Place one tablespoon mixture in center of each square. Bring up corners; seal edges to within I inch of top. Fold back points to make an opening in the top. Place in greased 11x7-inch pan. Bake at 400° for 20 to 25 minutes until golden brown. Serve warm with Milk Sauce.

Milk Sauce: In medium saucepan, combine sugar, flour and salt. Gradually add milk, stir until smooth; add butter. Bring to a boil over medium heat, stirring constantly. Boil I minute. Remove from heat; add vanilla.

Tips: Substitute Pillsbury Refrigerated Turnover Pastries for biscuit base. Use fruit mixture in place of cinnamon filling in each roll. Bake at 400° for 18 to 20 minutes. Add icing to Milk Sauce.

I tablespoon preserves or canned pie filling may be substituted for the cinnamon filling in each roll.

*For use with Pillsbury's Best Self-Rising Flour, omit baking powder and salt.

Pineapple cream-puff mounted on a buttery crust and drizzled with creamy icing — a new twist to "Kringle." Deliciously rich coffee complement. Make ahead, bake later, if you like.

Swedish Pineapple Pastries

Crust
>   ¼ cup butter or margarine
>   2 tablespoons water
>   ¾ cup Pillsbury's Best All Purpose or
>   Self-Rising Flour

Pineapple Filling
>   1 cup water
>   ½ cup butter or margarine
>   1 cup Pillsbury's Best All Purpose or
>   Self-Rising Flour
>   3 eggs
>   ½ cup pineapple preserves
>   1 teaspoon almond extract

Icing
>   1 cup confectioners' sugar
>   2 tablespoons light cream
>   ¼ teaspoon almond extract
>   Almond slices, if desired

OVEN 375°   14 TO 16 PASTRIES

Crust: In medium saucepan, heat butter and water over medium heat until butter is melted. Remove from heat. Add flour all at once; stir until mixture forms ball. Divide dough in half. With back of spoon or fingers press out onto ungreased cookie sheet to form two 12x3-inch rectangles. Spread Filling to within ½-inch of edges. Bake at 375° for 25 to 30 minutes until light golden brown. Cool slightly; drizzle with Icing; sprinkle with almonds. Serve warm, cut in strips.

Pineapple Filling: In medium saucepan, bring water and butter to rolling boil. Add flour all at once; cook over medium heat, stirring constantly until mixture forms stiff ball. Remove from heat. Add eggs, one at a time, beating vigorously after each until mixture is smooth and glossy. Stir in preserves and almond extract.

Icing: Combine confectioners' sugar, cream and almond extract until smooth and creamy.

Tips: Prepare ahead up to baking point, cover and refrigerate. Place in oven 45 minutes before serving time.

For individual pastries, divide crust dough into 16 pieces. Press each into individual 3-inch rectangles or rounds. Top with rounded tablespoon of filling.

Pineapple preserves, baked on the cake, under a spicy crumb layer, make a moist and marvelous dessert. Top it off with a whipped topping. An easy one-step cake.

Hawaiian Holiday Dessert

>   1 cup Pillsbury's Best All Purpose Flour*
>   ⅓ cup sugar
>   1½ teaspoons baking powder
>   ½ teaspoon salt
>   ¼ cup shortening
>   ⅓ cup milk
>   1 egg
>   1 teaspoon vanilla
>   ½ cup pineapple preserves

Topping
>   2 tablespoons butter or margarine
>   ¼ cup sugar
>   ¼ cup Pillsbury's Best All Purpose Flour
>   ½ teaspoon cinnamon

OVEN 350°   8 TO 10 SERVINGS

In small mixer bowl, combine flour, sugar, baking powder and salt. Add shortening, milk, egg and vanilla. Blend at lowest speed until moistened; beat at medium speed 2 minutes. Spread on bottom of greased and floured 8-inch square pan. Spread preserves over batter; sprinkle with Topping. Bake at 350° for 25 to 30 minutes until top springs back when touched lightly in center. Serve warm, cut in squares, with whipped cream, if desired.

Topping: In small saucepan, melt butter. Remove from heat. Mix in sugar, flour and cinnamon until crumbly.

Like a pudding-cake made with hot rhubarb sauce. A tangy treat hot or cold, and easily made in just an hour.

Last Minute Dessert

> 1 egg, beaten
> 1 cup Pillsbury's Best All Purpose Flour*
> 1 cup sugar
> 2 teaspoons baking powder
> ½ teaspoon salt
> ¼ cup milk
> 2 tablespoons cooking oil
> 2 cups hot Rhubarb Sauce page 11

OVEN 400°   8 SERVINGS

In large mixing bowl, combine all ingredients, except Rhubarb Sauce. Stir until well blended. Spread in 9-inch square pan which has been greased on the bottom only. Cover batter with Rhubarb Sauce. Bake at 400° for 25 to 30 minutes until golden brown. Serve warm with whipped cream.

Tip: To substitute frozen rhubarb for Rhubarb Sauce, combine 1 package (1 lb.) frozen rhubarb and 1 cup boiling water in small saucepan. Return mixture to boiling point over high heat, separating fruit with fork.

*For use with Pillsbury's Best Self-Rising Flour, omit baking powder and salt.

HIGH ALTITUDE ADJUSTMENT — 5,200 FEET. Reduce baking powder to 1 teaspoon.

Under the nut-sprinkled crust is a butterscotch pudding-cake with a cinnamon accent. Serve warm in an hour and a half, with whipped cream.

Cinnamon Pudding Cake

Cake
> 2 cups Pillsbury's Best All Purpose Flour*
> 1 cup sugar
> 2 teaspoons baking powder
> ½ teaspoon salt
> 2 to 3 teaspoons cinnamon
> 2 tablespoons shortening
> 1 cup milk
> ½ cup chopped walnuts

Sauce
> 1¾ cups firmly packed brown sugar
> 1½ cup water
> 2 tablespoons butter or margarine

OVEN 350°   8 TO 10 SERVINGS

Cake: In large mixing bowl, combine all Cake ingredients except walnuts; beat at medium speed until well blended. Spread in a 9-inch square pan which has been greased on the bottom only. Pour hot Sauce over Cake; sprinkle with walnuts. Bake at 350° for 35 to 40 minutes until top springs back when touched lightly in center. Serve warm with whipped cream.

Sauce: Combine all ingredients in saucepan. Bring to boil.

*For use with Pillsbury's Best Self-Rising Flour, omit baking powder and salt.

An easy brownie mix figures in this darkly fudgy pudding-cake that can be prepared and baked in an hour and fifteen minutes.

Marsh-Mocha Puddin' Cake

> ⅓ cup firmly packed brown sugar
> 2 tablespoons cocoa
> 1 cup hot coffee
> 2 cups miniature marshmallows

Brownie Topping
> 1 package (Regular Size) Pillsbury Walnut
>   Brownie Mix
> ⅔ cup dairy sour cream

OVEN 325°   8 SERVINGS

Combine brown sugar, cocoa and coffee in 8-inch square pan; blend well. Sprinkle with marshmallows. Spoon Brownie Topping over marshmallows, leaving some uncovered for a marbled top. Bake at 325° for 50 to 55 minutes. Serve warm or cold, with whipped cream.

Brownie Topping: In large mixing bowl, combine brownie mix and sour cream; stir until well blended. Batter will be stiff.

Tip: For coffee, 1 rounded teaspoonful instant coffee in 1 cup hot water may be used.

HIGH ALTITUDE ADJUSTMENT — Follow brownie mix package recommendations.

35

Baked Apple Cuplets

¼ cup sugar
½ teaspoon cinnamon
6 medium baking apples, peeled and cored
⅔ cup Pillsbury's Best All Purpose Flour*
⅔ cup sugar
¼ teaspoon baking powder
⅛ teaspoon salt
3 tablespoons cooking oil or melted butter
I teaspoon vanilla
I egg

OVEN 375°   6 SERVINGS

Combine sugar and cinnamon. Roll apples in sugar mixture; place in buttered 8-oz. custard cups. Spoon remaining sugar-cinnamon mixture in center of apples. In mixing bowl, combine flour, ⅔ cup sugar, baking powder and salt. Combine oil, vanilla and egg; add to dry ingredients; mix well. Spoon about 2 tablespoons of batter over each apple. Bake at 375° for 40 to 45 minutes or until apples are tender. Serve warm.

Tip: Reheat by wrapping in foil and placing in 350° oven for I5 minutes.

*For use with Pillsbury's Best Self-Rising Flour, omit baking powder and salt.

Brown - sugar - packed apples, individually wrapped in Cheddar crusts, sauced to a fare-thee-well and served warm and aromatic.

Glazed Apple Dumplings

I package Pillsbury Pie Crust Sticks or Mix
I cup shredded Cheddar cheese
6 medium baking apples, peeled and cored
⅓ cup firmly packed brown sugar
    Cinnamon
Sauce
⅔ cup firmly packed brown sugar
I½ cups water
2 tablespoons butter or margarine

OVEN 425°   6 DUMPLINGS

Prepare pie crust sticks or mix as directed on package for double crust, combining the cheese with the dry mix. Roll out on floured surface to a I2x18-inch rectangle. Cut into six 6-inch squares. Place apple in center of each. Fill cavities with brown sugar; sprinkle with

cinnamon. Bring points to center; seal edges. Place in I3x9-inch pan. Pour Sauce around dumplings. Bake at 425° for 45 to 50 minutes or until apples are tender. Baste with syrup; return to oven for 5 minutes more. Serve warm.

Sauce: In saucepan, combine all ingredients. Bring to rolling boil.

Tip: If apples are large, make 4 dumplings by rolling dough to a I4x14-inch rectangle. Cut into four 7-inch squares. Bake in 9-inch square pan.

A nut-crumb topping gives a rugged look to this buttermilk gingerbread recipe. Ready for hungry ranch hands in forty-five minutes. Leftovers make good lunch box snacks.

Western Gingerbread

2 cups Pillsbury's Best All Purpose Flour*
I¼ cups sugar
I teaspoon baking powder
2 teaspoons cinnamon
I½ teaspoons ginger
¼ teaspoon salt
½ cup shortening
I cup buttermilk or sour milk
2 tablespoons molasses
I teaspoon soda
I egg
½ cup chopped nuts

OVEN 350°   I3X9-INCH CAKE

In small mixer bowl, combine flour, sugar, baking powder, cinnamon, ginger and salt. Add shortening and mix at lowest speed until particles are fine. Remove ½ cup of crumbs; reserve for topping. Add buttermilk, molasses, soda, and egg to remaining crumb mixture. Blend until moistened, beat at medium speed for 2 minutes. Pour into I3x9-inch pan which has been greased on the bottom only. Sprinkle with nuts, then reserved crumb mixture. Bake at 350° for 25 to 30 minutes until cake springs back when touched lightly in center. Serve warm or cold cut in squares. Top with whipped cream, if desired.

Tips: To sour milk, see page 9.

Flaked coconut may be substituted for nuts in topping.

*For use with Pillsbury's Best Self-Rising Flour, omit baking powder, salt and soda.

An upside-down gingerbread ring highlighted with frozen lemonade glaze. The blanched almond and coconut topping give it texture appeal.

Lemon Ginger Ring

<u>Topping</u>
- ¼ cup butter or margarine
- ¼ cup firmly packed brown sugar
- 2 tablespoons frozen lemonade concentrate
- ½ cup flaked coconut
- 12 whole blanched almonds

<u>Gingerbread</u>
- 1 ½ cups Pillsbury's Best All Purpose Flour*
- ½ cup sugar
- 1 teaspoon soda
- ½ teaspoon cinnamon
- ½ teaspoon ginger
- ½ teaspoon allspice
- ¼ teaspoon salt
- ½ cup milk
- ⅓ cup shortening
- ⅓ cup light molasses
- 1 egg
- 2 tablespoons frozen lemonade concentrate

OVEN 350°   8 TO 10 SERVINGS

<u>Topping:</u> Melt butter in 6½-cup ring mold in oven. Sprinkle brown sugar, lemonade concentrate and coconut over butter. Mix just to combine. Arrange almonds over coconut mixture, pressing to bottom of pan. Pour Gingerbread over topping. Bake at 350° for 30 to 35 minutes until top springs back when touched lightly. Loosen edges with spatula. Invert onto serving plate; let stand 2 minutes, then remove pan. Serve warm with whipped cream or Lemon Whipped Cream page 10.

<u>Gingerbread:</u> In small mixer bowl blend all ingredients at lowest speed. Beat 2 minutes at medium speed.

*For use with Pillsbury's Best Self-Rising Flour, omit soda and salt.

HIGH ALTITUDE ADJUSTMENT — 5,200 FEET. Reduce soda to ½ teaspoon.

Family Dessert Favorites

● To many families, a meal isn't a meal without dessert. Here is a collection of simple and varied desserts that taste good and will be welcomed by everyone. Who doesn't associate home with moist cakes, crowned with imaginative toppings; squares of bar-type yummies which brother and sister measure carefully to see whose is bigger; fruity upside down cakes served warm or cold; steamed puddings with a snappy sauce; crisps and fruits with crunchy toppings? They're all here: dessert ideas for big families and small families, for mothers with leisure or little time, for Sunday best or any weekday. Everybody loves desserts.

Little drop shortcakes, made unusual with mashed bananas, split and served with cinnamon whipped cream and bananas. Thirty to forty-five minutes to prepare.

Quick Banana Buns

Banana Buns
  2¼ cups Pillsbury's Best All Purpose Flour*
  ½ cup firmly packed brown sugar
  ¼ cup sugar
  2 teaspoons baking powder
  1 teaspoon salt
  ¾ teaspoon soda
  ½ teaspoon cinnamon
  ¼ teaspoon nutmeg
  1 cup (2 medium) mashed banana
  ⅔ cup shortening
  ⅓ cup buttermilk or sour milk
  1 egg

Cinnamon Whipped Cream
  1 cup whipping cream
  1 tablespoon sugar
  ½ teaspoon vanilla
  ⅛ teaspoon cinnamon

OVEN 400°   14 TO 16 BUNS

<u>Banana Buns:</u> In large mixer bowl, combine all Banana Bun ingredients. Blend at low speed for 3 minutes. Drop by rounded tablespoonfuls, 3 inches apart, on greased cookie sheets. Bake at 400° for 15 to 20 minutes, until golden brown. While warm, split and serve with Cinnamon Whipped Cream and sliced bananas.

<u>Cinnamon Whipped Cream:</u> In small mixer bowl, combine all ingredients. Beat at high speed until thick.

<u>Tips:</u> *Make the banana buns ahead. Reheat by wrapping in foil and placing in 350° oven for 10 to 15 minutes.*

For luncheon muffins, drop batter by tablespoonfuls into 16 greased muffin cups.

*For use with Pillsbury's Best Self-Rising Flour, omit baking powder, soda and salt.

40

A three-flavor melody — rhubarb, pineapple and mint — served in squares with a crunchy topping. Tastes like Spring any time of year.

Saucy Perk-up Pudding

I package (1 lb.) frozen rhubarb, thaw, drain and reserve ¼ cup of syrup
1 can (1 lb. 4 oz.) crushed pineapple, drained
1 teaspoon dried mint leaves or ¼ teaspoon mint extract, if desired
1 egg
⅓ cup sugar
2 tablespoons flour
1 tablespoon lemon juice

Topping
1 cup Pillsbury's Best All Purpose Flour*
½ cup sugar
¼ teaspoon salt
½ cup butter or margarine

OVEN 375°   8 SERVINGS

In greased 8-inch square pan, combine rhubarb, pineapple and mint leaves. In small mixing bowl, blend egg, sugar, flour, rhubarb syrup and lemon juice at low speed for 2 minutes; pour over fruit. Sprinkle on Topping. Bake at 375° for 40 to 45 minutes until golden brown and bubbly. Cut into squares and serve plain or with whipped cream.

Topping: In small mixing bowl, combine flour, sugar and salt. Cut in butter until mixture is crumbly.

Tip: 2 cups cut-up fresh rhubarb may be used. Increase first measure of sugar to ¾ cup and omit rhubarb syrup.

*For use with Pillsbury's Best Self-Rising Flour, omit salt.

Swirls of peach preserves and coconut appear as you slice this rich and easy roll-up. Start early enough to chill.

Easy Peach Strudel

2¼ cups Pillsbury's Best All Purpose or Self Rising Flour
1 cup dairy sour cream
1 cup butter, softened
2 cups peach preserves
1 cup flaked coconut
8 tablespoons finely chopped walnuts

OVEN 450°   ABOUT 32 SLICES

In large mixing bowl, combine flour, sour cream and butter; blend well. Cover; chill at least 1 hour. Roll out dough, one-fourth at a time, to a 12x8-inch rectangle on a well-floured surface. Spread with ½ cup preserves to within 1 inch of edges. Sprinkle with ¼ cup coconut and 2 tablespoons walnuts. Starting with 12-inch side, roll up jelly roll fashion. Seal edges and ends. Place, seam-side down, on ungreased cookie sheet. Repeat with remaining dough to make 4 rolls. Bake at 450° for 18 to 20 minutes. Cool. Sprinkle with confectioners' sugar. Cut into slices.

Tip: Keep a baked roll of strudel in the freezer for unexpected coffee guests. It will thaw quickly after slicing.

Squares of pumpkin plus mincemeat for an exciting fall combination sandwiched between crunchy crust with corn flakes and oatmeal.

Pumpkin Plus Dessert

1 cup Pillsbury's Best All Purpose Flour*
1 cup quick-cooking rolled oats
1 cup corn flakes
⅓ cup firmly packed brown sugar
½ teaspoon soda
½ cup butter or margarine
2 cups prepared mincemeat
1 can (1 lb. 14 oz.) pumpkin pie mix
2 eggs
½ teaspoon cinnamon
¼ teaspoon nutmeg

OVEN 375°   12 TO 15 SERVINGS

In large mixing bowl, combine flour, rolled oats, corn flakes, brown sugar and soda. Cut in butter until particles are coarse. Reserve 1 cup crumb mixture. Press remaining mixture into bottom of ungreased 13x9-inch pan. Spread mincemeat over crumb mixture. In large mixing bowl, combine remaining ingredients. Pour over mincemeat; sprinkle with reserved crumb mixture. Bake at 375° for 40 to 45 minutes until knife inserted in center comes out clean. Cool. Served with whipped cream.

Tip: This pumpkin pie mix is pumpkin with sugar, spices and liquid added.

*For use with Pillsbury's Best Self-Rising Flour, omit soda.

Apples and crushed peanut brittle take to each other like old friends. Delicious, under a cinnamon crumb topping, served warm or cold.

Apple Candy Crisp

   6 cups (5 to 6 medium) peeled, sliced apples
  ¾ cup (¼ lb.) crushed peanut brittle
  ¼ cup sugar
  ½ teaspoon salt
   1 tablespoon lemon juice
  ¼ cup water

Topping
  ¾ cup Pillsbury's Best All Purpose Flour*
  ½ cup sugar
   1 teaspoon cinnamon
  ¼ cup butter or margarine, melted

OVEN 400°   4 TO 6 SERVINGS

Combine apples, peanut brittle, sugar, salt and lemon juice in greased 8-inch square pan or 1½-quart casserole. Sprinkle Topping mixture over apples; drizzle with water. Bake at 400° 30 to 35 minutes until golden brown and apples are tender. Spoon into serving dishes and serve warm or cold with plain or whipped cream.

Topping: In small mixing bowl, combine flour, sugar and cinnamon; add melted butter and mix well.

Tip: 1 can of prepared apple pie filling may be used for filling, omitting sugar and salt.

*For use with Pillsbury's Best Self-Rising Flour, omit salt.

Lemon filling spread on a crunchy base made with dry coconut almond frosting mix, and topped with crumbs of the same. Serve cool squares to family or guests.

Tropical Crunch

   1 package Pillsbury Coconut-Almond
     Frosting Mix
  ½ cup Pillsbury's Best All Purpose Flour*
  ½ cup (12) finely crushed soda crackers
  ½ teaspoon soda
  ⅓ cup butter or margarine
   1 package (3½ oz.) lemon pudding and
     pie filling mix

OVEN 350°   9 SERVINGS

In large mixing bowl, combine dry frosting mix, flour, crackers and soda. Cut in butter

until mixture is the size of small peas. Press half into bottom of 8-inch square pan. Prepare pie filling according to package directions, omitting ¼ cup of the water. Pour hot mixture over crumb base. Sprinkle with remaining crumb mixture. Bake at 350° for 20 to 30 minutes until golden brown. Cool. Cut into squares and serve with whipped cream; garnish with a thin slice of lemon.

Tip: For a more distinct lemon flavor, add a teaspoon of grated lemon peel to pudding after cooking.

*For use with Pillsbury's Best Self-Rising Flour, omit soda.

Cereal flakes play the role traditionally given to oatmeal in the butter-crumb top and bottom layers. Juicy peach slices give it a golden warmth.

Peach Elizabeth

   1 cup Pillsbury's Best All Purpose Flour*
  ½ cup firmly packed brown sugar
  ½ cup crushed corn flakes or other dry
     cereal flakes
  ½ teaspoon soda
  ½ teaspoon salt
  ½ teaspoon cinnamon
  ¼ teaspoon nutmeg
   1 teaspoon grated lemon peel
   1 teaspoon lemon juice
  ½ cup butter or margarine, softened
   1 can (1 lb. 13 oz.) peach slices, drained

OVEN 350°   9 SERVINGS

In large mixer bowl, combine all ingredients except peaches. Mix at low speed until crumbly and well blended. Press half of mixture into bottom of greased 8-inch square pan. Arrange peach slices over mixture in pan. Sprinkle on remaining crumb mixture. Bake at 350° for 45 to 50 minutes, until golden brown. Serve warm or cold with whipped cream.

*For use with Pillsbury's Best Self-Rising Flour, omit soda, salt and lemon juice.

Pretty cherry pie filling peeks through crumbly topping. Underneath is a surprising cookie crust.

Cherry Nut Crunch

   2 cups Pillsbury's Best All Purpose Flour*
½ cup sugar
½ teaspoon soda
½ teaspoon cream of tartar
½ teaspoon salt
½ cup butter or margarine, softened
  1 egg
  1 tablespoon grated lemon peel
  1 teaspoon vanilla
  1 can (1 lb. 5 oz.) prepared cherry pie filling
¼ cup chopped nuts

Topping

  ½ cup Pillsbury's Best All Purpose or Self-Rising Flour
¼ cup sugar
  3 tablespoons butter or margarine

OVEN 350°   10-INCH PIE

In large mixer bowl, combine flour, sugar, soda, cream of tartar, salt, butter, egg, lemon peel and vanilla. Mix at low speed until well blended. Press mixture into greased 10-inch pie pan or 9-inch round layer pan. Do not cover rim of pan. Spoon on cherry pie filling. Sprinkle with Topping and nuts. Bake at 350° for 35 to 40 minutes until golden brown. Serve plain or with ice cream.

Topping: In small mixing bowl, combine flour and sugar. Cut in butter until mixture is crumbly.

Tip: For variety, substitute other prepared pie fillings such as blueberry or pineapple for the cherry filling.

*For use with Pillsbury's Best Self-Rising Flour, omit soda, cream of tartar and salt.

Under each pink frozen topping is a crumb crust square made with red raspberry rhubarb sauce. Make topping ahead and freeze. Give yourself an hour and a half for the rest.

Ruby Razz Crunch

   1 package (1 lb.) frozen rhubarb, thaw, drain and reserve syrup
   1 package (10 oz.) frozen raspberries, thaw, drain, reserve syrup and ¼ cup raspberries
½ cup sugar
  3 tablespoons cornstarch
1½ cups Pillsbury's Best All Purpose or Self-Rising Flour
  1 cup firmly packed brown sugar
  1 cup quick-cooking rolled oats
  1 teaspoon cinnamon
½ cup butter or margarine, melted

Pink Frozen Cream Topping

  1 cup whipping cream
¼ cup sugar
   Reserved ¼ cup of raspberries
  1 to 3 drops red food coloring, if desired

OVEN 325°   8 TO 10 SERVINGS

Combine drained syrups, measure 1 cup, adding water if necessary. In saucepan, combine sugar and cornstarch; stir in fruit syrups. Cook, stirring constantly, until thick. In large mixing bowl, combine flour, brown sugar, rolled oats and cinnamon. Add melted butter; mix well. Press two-thirds crumb mixture in greased 9-inch square pan. Spoon on fruit and thickened juices. Sprinkle on remaining crumbs. Bake at 325° for 55 to 60 minutes until golden brown and bubbly. Serve warm or cold with Pink Frozen Cream Topping.

Pink Frozen Cream Topping: Beat whipping cream until slightly thickened. Add sugar and reserved raspberries; continue beating until thick. Drop in mounds on waxed paper; freeze until firm.

Tip: If desired, use all of the raspberries in the dessert and omit the cream topping. Serve with cream or ice cream.

Press tender cream cheese crusts in muffin cups, line with chopped pecans, fill with pineapple filling. Cookie tarts—serve with whipped cream.

Southern Pineapple Tarts

Pastry

    ½ cup butter, softened
     I package (3 oz.) cream cheese, softened
     2 tablespoons sugar
    I½ cups Pillsbury's Best All Purpose Flour*
    ¾ cup chopped pecans

Filling

     2 eggs
     I cup firmly packed brown sugar
     I can (8 oz.) crushed pineapple, drained
       (⅔ cup)
     2 tablespoons butter or margarine, melted

OVEN 350°   I2 TARTS

<u>Pastry</u>: In small mixer bowl, combine butter, cream cheese and sugar. Mix at low speed until well blended. Add flour; mix thoroughly. Form into a ball. Cover and chill 30 minutes. Press chilled dough into bottom and up sides of I2 muffin cups. Sprinkle ½ cup of the chopped pecans in bottom of pastry-lined cups. Spoon Filling over pecans. Sprinkle remaining pecans on top. Bake at 350° for 30 to 35 minutes until golden brown. Cool I5 minutes before removing from pan. Cool completely. Serve with whipped cream, if desired.

<u>Filling</u>: In small mixing bowl, combine eggs, brown sugar, pineapple and melted butter. Stir until well blended.

*Self-Rising Flour is not recommended for use in this recipe.

Little walnut-coconut pies in dainty muffin cup pastries. Or make it a full 9-inch pie. Top it off with cool whipped cream.

Nut Basket Tarts

Double Crust Pastry, see page 62

3 eggs
1¼ cups firmly packed brown sugar
2 tablespoons flour
1 teaspoon salt
½ teaspoon baking powder
1 cup chopped nuts
½ cup flaked coconut

OVEN 350°   14 TO 16 TARTS

Prepare pastry. Divide dough into two portions. Roll out each portion on lightly floured surface to ⅛-inch thickness. Cut with 4½-inch round cutter; fit loosely into muffin cups, pressing into place.

In small mixer bowl, combine eggs, brown sugar, flour, salt and baking powder. Beat at high speed until well blended. Stir in nuts and coconut. Spoon into pastry-lined muffin pans. Bake at 350° for 20 to 25 minutes until filling is set. Cool; remove from pan. Serve with whipped cream.

Tip: Recipe may be made in 9-inch pie pan. Prepare unbaked pastry shell, see page 63. Pour in filling. Bake at 350° for 30 to 35 minutes.

Moist cake bakes up around cinnamon sugared peaches. Prepared peach pie filling makes it easy for a family supper.

Peach Buckle

1 cup Pillsbury's Best All Purpose Flour*
½ cup sugar
1 teaspoon baking powder
¼ teaspoon salt
⅓ cup butter or margarine, softened
2 eggs
1 can (1 lb. 5 oz.) prepared peach pie
   filling
2 tablespoons sugar
½ teaspoon cinnamon

OVEN 350°   6 TO 8 SERVINGS

In small mixer bowl, combine flour, sugar, baking powder, salt, butter and eggs. Blend at low speed until dry ingredients are moistened; beat at high speed 2 minutes. Turn batter into greased and floured 9-inch square pan. Spread over bottom and sides. Top with peach filling. Sprinkle on mixture of sugar and cinnamon. Bake at 350° for 45 to 50 minutes until golden brown. Serve warm or cold with ice cream or whipped cream.

Tip: If desired, use 1 can (1 lb. 14 oz.) peach slices, drained. Combine slices with ½ cup sugar, 2 tablespoons flour and ½ teaspoon cinnamon.

*For use with Pillsbury's Best Self-Rising Flour, omit baking powder and salt.

Individual cheese rounds with apple filling middles. A perfect not-too-sweet dessert. An hour and fifteen minutes 'til tart-eatin' time.

Apple 'N Cheese Tarts

2 cups Pillsbury's Best All Purpose Flour*
2 cups shredded Cheddar cheese
½ teaspoon salt
½ cup butter or margarine
⅓ cup milk
1 can (1 lb. 5 oz.) prepared apple pie
   filling
¼ cup raisins

OVEN 400°   18 TO 24 TARTS

In large mixing bowl, combine flour, shredded cheese and salt. Cut in butter until particles are the size of small peas. Sprinkle milk over mixture, stirring with fork until dough holds together. Form into a ball; wrap in waxed paper and chill ½ hour. Roll out dough on floured surface to ⅛-inch thickness. Cut into rounds with floured 3-inch cutter. Place half of rounds on ungreased cookie sheet. In small mixing bowl, combine apple pie filling and raisins. Place a spoonful of filling in center of each round. Cut a cross in center of remaining rounds and place over filling. Seal edges. Bake at 400° for 12 to 15 minutes until golden brown.

Tip: To reheat, place on cookie sheet and heat in 350° oven for 10 minutes.

*For use with Pillsbury's Best Self-Rising Flour, omit salt.

Spicy apple filling has a crumb-crust bed and a sour-cream blanket sprinkled with sugar and nutmeg. Apples never had it so good. Serve warm, in one hour plus.

Cream Crowned Apple Dessert

Crumb Crust
1½ cups Pillsbury's Best All Purpose Flour*
¼ cup firmly packed brown sugar
½ teaspoon salt
¼ teaspoon baking powder
⅓ cup butter or margarine
   Sugar
   Nutmeg

Filling
   1 can (15 oz.) prepared apple pie filling
½ teaspoon nutmeg
   1 tablespoon lemon juice

Topping
   1 egg, beaten
   1 cup dairy sour cream
   1 tablespoon firmly packed brown sugar
   1 teaspoon grated lemon peel

OVEN 400°   9 SERVINGS

Crumb Crust: In mixing bowl, combine flour, sugar, salt and baking powder. Cut in butter until particles are fine. Press firmly onto bottom of 9-inch square pan. Cover with Filling; spread with Topping. Sprinkle with sugar and nutmeg. Bake at 400° for 35 to 40 minutes until lightly browned. Cool.

Filling: Combine all ingredients; mix well.

Topping: Combine all ingredients; mix well.

*For use with Pillsbury's Best Self-Rising Flour, omit salt and baking powder.

Split squares of a good banana-nut cake, filled and topped with whipped cream and banana slices. Delicious warm or cold.

Banana Split Shortcake

1¼ cups Pillsbury's Best All Purpose Flour*
   1 cup sugar
   1 teaspoon soda
½ teaspoon salt
   1 cup (2 medium) mashed bananas
½ cup shortening
¼ cup milk
   2 eggs
   1 cup chopped nuts

OVEN 350°   8 TO 10 SERVINGS

In large mixer bowl, combine flour, sugar, soda, salt, mashed bananas, shortening, milk and eggs. Blend at low speed until dry ingredients are moistened; beat at medium speed for 3 minutes. Stir in nuts. Pour into greased and floured 9-inch square pan. Bake at 350° for 40 to 45 minutes until cake springs back when touched lightly in center. Cut in squares, split squares, fill and top with whipped cream and banana slices.

*For use with Pillsbury's Best Self-Rising Flour, decrease soda to ¼ teaspoon and omit salt.
*HIGH ALTITUDE ADJUSTMENT — 5,200 FEET.
Reduce soda to ½ teaspoon.*

Like a flat square pie with a lattice top, colorfully fruited with cranberries, strawberries and pineapple. Serve in squares as a dessert or snack.

Tasty Berry Gems

½ cup sugar
   1 tablespoon cornstarch
   1 cup cranberries
   1 can (8½ oz.) or 1 cup crushed pineapple, undrained
   1 package (10 oz.) frozen strawberries, thawed, drained
   1 teaspoon vanilla
   1 package Pillsbury Pie Crust Mix or Sticks
   Milk

OVEN 425°   10 TO 12 SERVINGS

In saucepan, combine sugar, cornstarch, cranberries, pineapple and strawberries. Cook over medium heat, stirring occasionally, until cranberries burst and liquid thickens. Stir in vanilla. Cool. Prepare pie crust mix for double crust pie as directed on package. Divide dough into two portions, one twice as large as the other. Place larger portion on ungreased cookie sheet. Roll out to a 14x11-inch rectangle. (Cookie sheet will not slip if placed on a damp cloth or paper towel.) Spread cooled filling to within ½ inch of edges. Brush uncovered edges with milk. Roll out remaining dough on floured surface. Cut into strips ½-inch wide; crisscross over filling to form lattice top. Brush lattice top with milk. Trim and fold up bottom crust to form a ½-inch rim; flute. Bake at 425° for 25 to 30 minutes until golden brown. Cool. Serve in squares topped with ice cream, if desired.

A crispy, crunchy torte filled with raspberries plays host to a mound of whipped cream colorfully bedazzled by clear red raspberry sauce.

Raspberry Walnut Torte

Torte
- 1 cup Pillsbury's Best All Purpose or Self-Rising Flour*
- ⅓ cup confectioners' sugar
- ½ cup butter, softened
- 1 package (10 oz.) frozen raspberries, thawed
- ¾ cup chopped walnuts
- 2 eggs
- 1 cup sugar
- ¼ cup Pillsbury's Best All Purpose Flour*
- ½ teaspoon baking powder
- ½ teaspoon salt
- 1 teaspoon vanilla

Raspberry Sauce
- ½ cup sugar
- 2 tablespoons cornstarch
- ½ cup water
- Reserved raspberry syrup
- 1 tablespoon lemon juice

OVEN 350°   9 SERVINGS

Torte: In small mixer bowl, combine 1 cup flour, confectioners' sugar and butter; blend well. Press into bottom of ungreased 9-inch square pan. Bake at 350° for 15 minutes. Cool. Drain raspberries; reserve liquid for Sauce. Spread berries over crust; sprinkle with walnuts. In small mixer bowl, combine eggs, sugar, ¼ cup flour, salt, baking powder and vanilla at low speed; blend well. Pour over walnuts. Bake at 350° for 35 to 40 minutes until golden brown. Cool. Cut into squares. Serve with whipped cream and Raspberry Sauce.

Raspberry Sauce: In small saucepan, combine all ingredients except lemon juice. Cook, stirring constantly, until thick and clear. Stir in lemon juice. Cool.

*For use with Pillsbury's Best Self-Rising Flour, omit baking powder and salt.

A good-old-days steamed Christmas pudding that smacks of all the raisins, nuts and spices memory can hold. Served with a wonderful nutmeg sauce.

My Mother's Pudding

Pudding
- 1½ cups Pillsbury's Best All Purpose Flour*
- 1½ teaspoons baking powder
- 1 teaspoon salt
- 1 teaspoon cinnamon
- ¾ teaspoon soda
- ½ teaspoon ground cloves
- ½ teaspoon nutmeg
- 1 cup raisins
- ¾ cup grated or ground suet
- ½ cup chopped nuts
- 1 egg
- ¾ cup milk
- ¾ cup molasses

Nutmeg Sauce
- ½ cup sugar
- 1 tablespoon cornstarch
- ½ teaspoon nutmeg
- 1¼ cups hot water
- ¼ cup butter, softened
- 1 teaspoon vanilla
- 1 egg yolk

STEAM 2 TO 2½ HOURS   10 SERVINGS

Pudding: In large mixer bowl, combine all Pudding ingredients. Mix at low speed 3 minutes. Pour into greased 2-quart mold, or two 1 lb. coffee cans. Cover tightly with aluminum foil. Place on rack in large kettle; add boiling water to one-third height of mold. Cover kettle tightly. Steam 2 to 2½ hours or until pudding springs back when lightly touched in center. Serve hot with Nutmeg Sauce.

Nutmeg Sauce: In top of double boiler, combine sauce ingredients. Beat with rotary beater until well blended. Cook over boiling water, stirring occasionally, until slightly thickened.

*For use with Pillsbury's Best Self-Rising Flour, omit baking powder and salt; decrease soda to ¼ teaspoon.

Delicious warm or cold — blueberry pie filling spooned over cake batter, spread with coconut meringue and baked. Serve cut in squares.

Triple Treat Blueberry Squares

- 1¼ cups Pillsbury's Best All Purpose Flour*
- ¾ cup sugar
- 1 teaspoon salt
- ½ teaspoon soda
- ½ cup water
- 2 egg yolks
- 2 tablespoons grated coconut

Filling
- 1 can (1 lb. 5 oz.) prepared blueberry pie filling
- 1 tablespoon flour
- 1 tablespoon grated lemon peel
- 2 tablespoons lemon juice

Topping
- 2 egg whites
- 1 tablespoon water
- ¼ teaspoon salt
- ⅓ cup sugar
- 1 cup grated coconut
- 2 tablespoons flour

OVEN 350°   10 TO 12 SERVINGS

In mixing bowl, combine flour, sugar, salt, soda, water and egg yolks; mix thoroughly. Spread in bottom of 13x9-inch pan which has been greased on the bottom only. Drop Filling by teaspoonfuls over batter. Spread Topping over Filling; sprinkle with coconut. Bake at 350° for 35 to 40 minutes until golden brown. Serve warm or cold, cut in squares.

Filling: In mixing bowl, combine all ingredients.

Topping: In small mixer bowl, combine egg whites, water and salt; beat until soft mounds form. Gradually add sugar; continue beating until stiff peaks form. Fold in coconut and flour.

*Not recommended for use with Pillsbury's Best Self-Rising Flour.

A flaming holiday coup de kitchen. Traditional plum pudding translated into orange marmalade and candied fruit. Lower the lights, and bring on the hard sauce, too.

Orange Festival Pudding

Pudding

    I cup Pillsbury's Best All Purpose Flour*
    1½ teaspoons soda
     I teaspoon salt
     ¼ teaspoon cinnamon
     ¼ teaspoon cloves
      3 cups soft bread crumbs
      I jar (12 oz.) or I cup orange marmalade
      I cup milk
      I cup chopped candied fruit
     ½ cup butter or margarine, melted

Hard Sauce

      2 cups confectioners' sugar
     ½ cup butter or margarine, softened
      I tablespoon boiling water
      2 teaspoons rum or brandy flavoring
      I teaspoon vanilla
     ⅛ teaspoon salt

STEAM 2½ TO 3 HOURS   10 TO 12 SERVINGS

Pudding: In large mixer bowl, combine Pudding ingredients. Mix at low speed until well blended. Pour into greased 7 or 8-cup mold; cover with tight cover or aluminum foil. Place on rack in large kettle; add boiling water to one-third height of mold. Cover kettle tightly. Steam for 2½ to 3 hours, or until top springs back when touched lightly in center. Serve warm with Hard Sauce.

Hard Sauce: In small mixer bowl, combine Sauce ingredients. Beat at high speed until well blended. Chill until serving time.

Tips: To flame, soak sugar cubes in orange or lemon extract, place around Pudding and ignite. Or, warm ¼ cup brandy in container with long flame-proof handle. Ignite. Pour over Pudding.

2 tablespoons rum or brandy may be used for flavorings in Hard Sauce.

For shaped Hard Sauce, press through cookie press onto cookie sheet, using tips for desired shape. Chill until serving time.

*For use with Pillsbury's Best Self-Rising Flour, decrease soda to I teaspoon and omit salt.

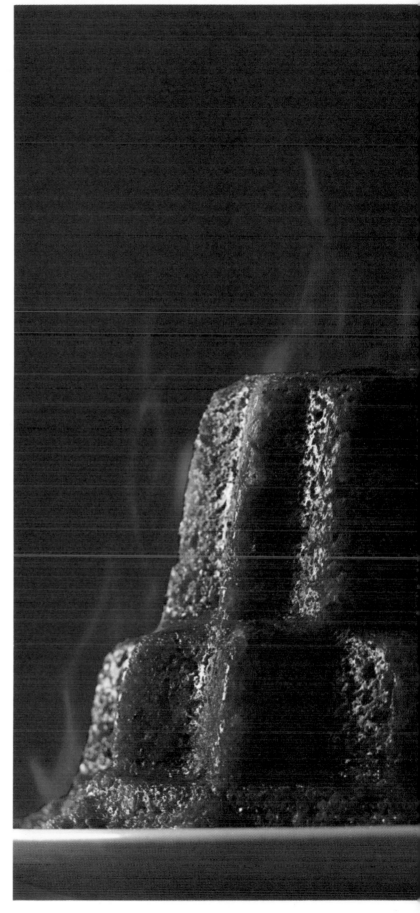

49

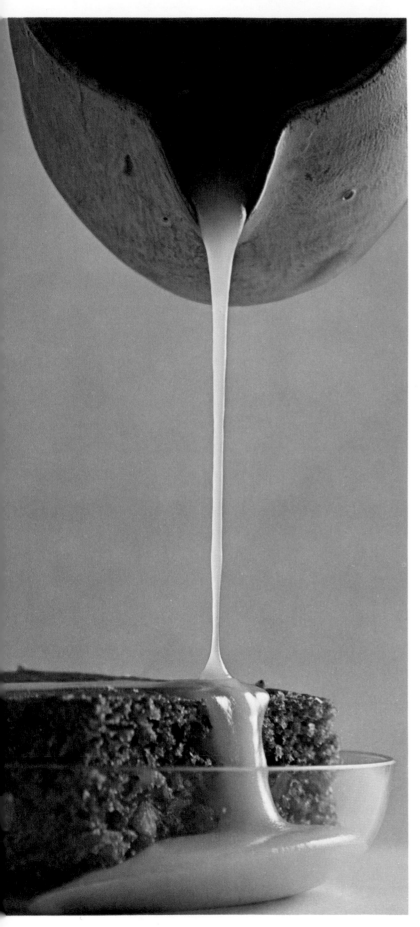

Plum-ful of prunes, nuts and spices and gilded with a rich buttermilk butter sauce. It's moist as a steamed pudding, but it is baked. Serve in an hour and a half, or reheat.

Sugarplum Cake

Cake

    2 cups Pillsbury's Best All Purpose Flour*
  1½ cups sugar
  2½ teaspoons baking powder
  1¼ teaspoons soda
    I teaspoon salt
    I teaspoon cinnamon
    I teaspoon nutmeg
    I teaspoon allspice
    I cup chopped nuts
    I cup cut-up cooked prunes
    I cup buttermilk
   ¾ cup cooking oil
    3 eggs

Butter Sauce

    I cup sugar
    2 tablespoons cornstarch
   ½ cup buttermilk
   ½ cup butter or margarine
    I teaspoon vanilla

OVEN 350°   13x9-INCH CAKE

Cake: In large mixer bowl, combine Cake ingredients. Mix at low speed for 3 minutes. Spread batter in greased 13x9-inch pan. Bake at 350° for 35 to 40 minutes until cake springs back when touched lightly. Serve warm or cold with Butter Sauce.

Butter Sauce: In saucepan, combine sugar and cornstarch. Add buttermilk, butter and vanilla. Bring to rolling boil; boil I minute. Serve warm.

Tip: To reheat cake, cover with aluminum foil and place in 350° oven 15 minutes.

*For use with Pillsbury's Best Self-Rising Flour, omit baking powder and salt. Decrease soda to ½ teaspoon.

HIGH ALTITUDE ADJUSTMENT — 5,200 FEET.
Reduce baking powder to 1½ teaspoons, soda to I teaspoon. Bake at 350° for 40 to 45 minutes.

Invite your most avid chocolate fans for this steamed chocolate pudding served in moist rounds with hard sauce or ice cream and chocolate sauce. Make extra and freeze for later use.

Steamed Brownie Roll

 2 cups Pillsbury's Best All Purpose Flour*
 I cup sugar
 I teaspoon soda
½ teaspoon salt
 2 envelopes (I oz. each) premelted
  unsweetened chocolate
 I cup water
 I cup chopped dates
½ cup chopped nuts
¼ cup shortening
 I teaspoon vanilla
 I egg

STEAM I½ TO 2 HOURS IO TO I2 SERVINGS

In large mixing bowl, combine all ingredients. Mix until well blended. Spoon batter into greased I½-quart mold or three No. 2 cans. Cover with aluminum foil. Place on rack in large kettle; add boiling water to one-third height of cans. Cover kettle tightly. Steam for I½ to 2 hours or until top springs back when touched lightly in center. Serve warm with hard sauce or ice cream and chocolate sauce.

<u>Tips:</u> *To reheat, wrap in aluminum foil and place in 350° oven about 30 minutes.*

Make ahead and freeze. Thaw and then heat in 350° oven for about 30 minutes.

A No. 2 can holds approximately 2½ cups liquid and has a net weight of about I lb. 4 oz.

*For use with Pillsbury's Best Self-Rising Flour, omit soda and salt.

A moist and yummy upside-down cake made in a ring. Glazed topping of orange marmalade and coconut absolutely sparkles. An hour or less.

Orange Coconut Ring

<u>Orange Coconut Topping</u>
- ¼ cup butter or margarine
- ¾ cup orange marmalade
- ½ cup flaked coconut

<u>Cake</u>
- 1½ cups Pillsbury's Best All Purpose Flour*
- ½ cup sugar
- 2 teaspoons baking powder
- ¼ teaspoon salt
- ½ cup butter or margarine, softened
- ½ cup milk
- 1 tablespoon orange marmalade
- 2 eggs

OVEN 375°   8 TO 10 SERVINGS

<u>Orange Coconut Topping</u>: Melt butter in 9-inch ring mold in oven, add marmalade and coconut; mix well and spread evenly. Pour Cake batter over mixture. Bake at 375° for 35 to 45 minutes or until cake springs back when touched lightly. Cool 5 minutes; loosen edges with spatula. Invert onto serving plate. If desired, serve with whipped cream or ice cream.

<u>Cake</u>: In small mixer bowl, combine all ingredients at lowest speed; beat 2 minutes at medium speed.

*For use with Pillsbury's Best Self-Rising Flour, omit baking powder and salt.

HIGH ALTITUDE ADJUSTMENT — 5,200 FEET. Reduce baking powder to 1½ teaspoons.

A pretty caper with a cake mix. A fine and fancy dessert quickly made with pineapple pie filling hidden between a cake and frosting mix.

Pineapple Meringue Torte

- 1 package Pillsbury Yellow Batter Cake Mix
- 1 can (1 lb. 5 oz.) prepared pineapple pie filling
- 1 package Pillsbury Fluffy White Frosting Mix
- 2 tablespoons flaked coconut

OVEN 350°   13x9-INCH CAKE

Prepare and bake cake mix as directed on package for 13x9-inch cake. Cool 10 minutes. Spread pineapple filling over top. Prepare frosting mix as directed on package; spread over pineapple filling, sealing to edges. Sprinkle with coconut. Bake at 350° for 12 to 15 minutes until lightly browned.

Tip: Try this idea with other batter cake mix flavors and other pie filling flavors.

HIGH ALTITUDE ADJUSTMENT — Follow cake mix package recommendation.

Orange Coconut Ring

52

Dream of a coconut nut bar tartly frosted with lemon, and you've got the picture. Ready to cut in squares in about an hour.

Lemon Dream Dessert

⅓ cup butter or margarine
1 cup Pillsbury's Best All Purpose Flour*
2 tablespoons sugar
2 eggs
½ cup firmly packed brown sugar
¼ teaspoon salt
⅛ teaspoon baking powder
½ teaspoon vanilla
¾ cup flaked coconut
½ cup chopped walnuts

Lemon Frosting
1½ cups confectioners' sugar
2 tablespoons lemon juice
2 teaspoons grated lemon peel

OVEN 350°   8 TO 10 SERVINGS

In small mixer bowl, cut butter into flour and sugar until mixture is coarse and crumbly. Press into ungreased 9-inch square pan. Bake at 350° for 15 minutes until set but not brown. In same mixer bowl, combine eggs, brown sugar, salt, baking powder and vanilla. Mix at low speed until well blended. Stir in coconut and walnuts. Spread over partially baked crust. Bake at 350° for 20 to 25 minutes. Frost immediately. Cool and cut into bars or squares. *Lemon Frosting:* Combine all ingredients in small mixing bowl. Beat until smooth.

Tip: If desired, omit frosting and serve topped with ice cream or whipped cream.

*For use with Pillsbury's Best Self-Rising Flour, omit salt and baking powder.

Dessert squares that can also masquerade as bar cookies. Prepared apricot pie filling makes it forty minutes easy.

Apricot Dessert Bars

2 cups Pillsbury's Best All Purpose Flour*
1 cup sugar
1 teaspoon salt
½ teaspoon soda
¾ cup butter or margarine, softened
1½ cups flaked coconut
½ cup chopped walnuts
1 can (1 lb. 6 oz.) prepared apricot pie filling

OVEN 400°   12 TO 15 SERVINGS

In large mixer bowl, combine flour, sugar, salt, soda and butter. Mix at lowest speed until coarse and crumbly. Stir in coconut and walnuts. Press half the crumb mixture in bottom of greased 13x9-inch baking pan. Spread pie filling evenly over base; sprinkle remaining crumbs over top. Bake at 400° for 20 to 25 minutes until golden brown. Cool and cut into bars. If desired, serve with whipped cream.

*For use with Pillsbury's Best Self-Rising Flour, omit salt and soda.

Two-tone marble cake made from mix bakes over a spiced apple filling mix. Serve inverted — and still warm — in pretty squares. Only fifty minutes.

Marbapple Ginger Cake

Apple Fruit Filling
1 can (1 lb. 5 oz.) prepared apple pie filling
2 tablespoons butter or margarine, softened
1 tablespoon lemon juice
½ teaspoon cinnamon

Cake
1 package Pillsbury One Layer Yellow Batter Cake Mix
2 tablespoons molasses
½ teaspoon cinnamon
⅛ teaspoon nutmeg
1/16 teaspoon cloves

OVEN 350°   8 TO 10 SERVINGS

Apple Fruit Filling: In 9-inch square baking pan, combine pie filling, butter, lemon juice and cinnamon. Spoon light and dark Cake batters alternately over apple mixture. Bake at 350° for 40 to 45 minutes until cake springs back when touched lightly in center. Cool 5 to 10 minutes; loosen edges with spatula. Invert onto serving plate. Serve warm or cold, plain or with whipped cream.

Cake: Prepare cake mix as directed on package. Remove 1 cup batter to a small mixing bowl and stir in remaining ingredients.

Tip: Or, prepare Pillsbury Two-Layer Size Yellow Batter Cake Mix. Use half for cake batter above; bake remainder in cupcakes or layer. Freeze for later use.

HIGH ALTITUDE ADJUSTMENT — Follow cake mix package recommendations.

53

Juicy blueberries made snappy with cinnamon in this delicious one-step coffee cake. Serve for dessert or coffee klatch in an hour and a half.

Blueberry Boy Bait

    2 cups Pillsbury's Best All Purpose Flour*
1½ cups sugar
    2 teaspoons baking powder
    I teaspoon salt
⅔ cup butter or margarine, softened
    I cup milk
    2 eggs
    I cup blueberries, frozen, fresh or drained
      canned
¼ cup sugar
½ teaspoon cinnamon

OVEN 350°   13x9-INCH CAKE

In large mixer bowl, combine flour, sugar, baking powder, salt, butter, milk and eggs. Blend at low speed until dry ingredients are moistened; beat at medium speed for 3 minutes. Pour into greased and floured 13x9-inch pan. Arrange blueberries on top. Combine sugar and cinnamon; sprinkle over the top. Bake at 350° for 40 to 50 minutes or until cake springs back when touched lightly in center. Cut in squares and serve warm or cold with whipped cream or ice cream.

*For use with Pillsbury's Best Self-Rising Flour, omit baking powder and salt.

Bring out the apples, dates and raisins for this hearty spice cake served with ice cream and butterscotch sauce. An hour and a half.

New England Fruit Pudding

    I cup Pillsbury's Best All Purpose Flour*
⅔ cup sugar
¾ teaspoon soda
½ teaspoon salt
½ teaspoon cinnamon
¼ teaspoon nutmeg
½ cup shortening
  I tablespoon milk
  I egg
1½ cups shredded apples
½ cup cut-up dates
½ cup raisins

Butterscotch Sauce
½ cup sugar
½ cup firmly packed brown sugar
¼ cup light cream
 2 tablespoons corn syrup
¼ cup light cream
½ teaspoon vanilla

OVEN 350°   8 TO 10 SERVINGS

In large mixer bowl, combine flour, sugar, soda, salt, cinnamon, nutmeg, shortening, milk and egg. Blend at low speed until dry ingredients are moistened. (Mixture will be dry.) Add apples, dates and raisins; blend well. Spread in greased 8-inch square pan. Bake at 350° for 40 to 45 minutes or until top springs back when touched lightly in center. Serve warm with ice cream or whipped cream and Butterscotch Sauce.

Butterscotch Sauce: In saucepan, combine sugar, brown sugar, ¼ cup light cream and corn syrup. Cook over medium heat until a little syrup dropped in cold water forms a soft ball (234° F.). Cool slightly, stir in remaining ¼ cup light cream and vanilla.

Tip: Butterscotch ice cream topping may be used. Warm over hot water, thinning with cream if necessary.

*For use with Pillsbury's Best Self-Rising Flour, increase flour to 1¼ cups, decrease soda to ¼ teaspoon and omit salt.

Home-made caramel sauce smothers squares of brown sugar cake, loaded with walnuts and topped with ice cream. Serve warm or cold.

Walnut Sundae Torte

½ cup butter or margarine
  I to 2 cups chopped walnuts
  I cup firmly packed brown sugar
⅔ cup milk
  I teaspoon vanilla
  I egg
1½ cups Pillsbury's Best All Purpose Flour*
½ teaspoon soda
¼ teaspoon salt

Caramel Sauce
  I cup firmly packed brown sugar
½ cup light cream
¼ cup light corn syrup
¼ cup butter or margarine
½ teaspoon vanilla

OVEN 350°   8 TO 10 SERVINGS

In medium saucepan, melt butter over medium heat. Add walnuts and brown sugar; blend together until sugar is dissolved. Remove from heat. Mix in milk, vanilla and egg. Blend in flour, soda and salt until smooth. Pour into greased and floured 9-inch square pan. Bake at 350° for 25 to 30 minutes or until top springs back when touched lightly in center. Serve warm or cold, cut in squares and topped with ice cream and warm Caramel Sauce.

Caramel Sauce: In medium saucepan, combine brown sugar, cream, corn syrup and butter. Bring to rolling boil; boil 3 to 4 minutes, stirring occasionally. Remove from heat; stir in vanilla. Thin with a little cream if necessary.

Tip: Caramel ice cream topping may be used for Caramel Sauce. Warm over hot water.

*For use with Pillsbury's Best Self-Rising Flour, omit soda and salt.

Under the brown sugar sour cream topping is a rich moist date-nut-coconut torte that will melt in your mouth. Top it off with whipped cream or ice cream.

Bake-Off Date Torte

    I cup Pillsbury's Best All Purpose Flour*
    I cup graham cracker crumbs
    I teaspoon soda
    ½ teaspoon salt
    I cup cut-up dates
    ½ cup chopped nuts
    ½ cup flaked coconut
    ½ cup shortening
    ½ cup milk
    I teaspoon vanilla
    ¼ teaspoon orange extract
    2 eggs

Topping

    I cup firmly packed brown sugar
    ½ cup dairy sour cream
    I tablespoon cornstarch

OVEN 350°   12 TO 14 SERVINGS

In large mixer bowl, combine all ingredients, except Topping, at lowest speed until dry ingredients are moistened. Beat at high speed 3 minutes. Spread batter in greased 13x9-inch pan. Spread with Topping. Bake at 350° for 40 to 45 minutes until top springs back when touched lightly in center. Cut in squares and serve warm or cold with whipped cream or ice cream.

Topping: Combine brown sugar, sour cream and cornstarch.

*For use with Pillsbury's Best Self-Rising Flour, omit soda and salt.

A happy use of apples . . . teamed with nuts in a moist and mouthwatering cake. Good warm or cold. One hour.

Apple Ala Nut Torte

    3 eggs
    I teaspoon vanilla
    I cup firmly packed brown sugar
    ¾ cup Pillsbury's Best All Purpose Flour*
    I teaspoon baking powder
    ½ teaspoon salt
    2 cups (2 medium) finely chopped apples
    I cup chopped nuts

OVEN 350°   13x9-INCH CAKE

In large mixing bowl, beat eggs and vanilla until light; gradually add brown sugar, continuing to beat after each addition. Add flour, baking powder and salt; blend until dry ingredients are moistened. Stir in apples and nuts. Pour into greased and floured 13x9-inch pan. Bake at 350° for 25 to 30 minutes until top springs back when touched lightly in center. Serve warm or cold with whipped cream or ice cream.

*For use with Pillsbury's Best Self-Rising Flour, increase flour to I cup and omit baking powder and salt.

HIGH ALTITUDE ADJUSTMENT — 5,200 FEET. Bake at 350° for 30 to 35 minutes.

Apricots nested in a spongy cake, sprinkled with nuts, sugar and cinnamon. Serve warm or cold, cut in squares.

Apricot Dessert Cake

    2 eggs
    I can (I lb.) unpeeled apricot halves, drain
       and reserve ½ cup of syrup
    ¼ cup butter or margarine, melted
    ¼ teaspoon lemon extract
    1¼ cups Pillsbury's Best All Purpose Flour*
    ¾ cup sugar
    I teaspoon baking powder
    ¼ teaspoon salt
    ⅓ cup chopped nuts
    2 tablespoons sugar
    ½ teaspoon cinnamon

OVEN 350°   9-INCH SQUARE CAKE

In small mixer bowl, beat eggs at high speed until thick and ivory colored. Blend in reserved apricot syrup, butter and lemon extract. Add flour, sugar, baking powder and salt; blend on lowest speed just until thoroughly mixed. Pour into greased and floured 9-inch square pan. Arrange apricots, cut-side down, in rows on top of batter. Sprinkle with nuts. Combine sugar and cinnamon; sprinkle over batter. Bake at 350° for 25 to 30 minutes until top springs back when touched lightly in center. Serve warm or cold, cut in squares. Top with whipped cream, if desired.

*For use with Pillsbury's Best Self-Rising Flour, omit baking powder and salt.

HIGH ALTITUDE ADJUSTMENT — 5,200 FEET. Bake at 350° for 35 to 40 minutes.

Crunchy topping bakes atop this one-step pineapple cake. Then a yummy butter sauce is poured over warm cake to make it twice as delicious. One hour and fifteen minutes to prepare and bake.

Top Me Twice Cake

Cake
2 cups Pillsbury's Best All Purpose Flour*
1 cup sugar
1 teaspoon soda
1 teaspoon salt
1 can (13½ oz.) or 1½ cups crushed pineapple, undrained
1 teaspoon vanilla
2 eggs

Topping
½ cup firmly packed brown sugar
½ cup flaked coconut
½ cup chopped pecans

Sauce
½ cup butter or margarine
½ cup light cream
½ cup sugar
½ teaspoon vanilla

OVEN 350°   9-INCH SQUARE CAKE

Cake: In large mixer bowl, combine all Cake ingredients at lowest speed until blended; beat 2 minutes at medium speed. Pour into 9-inch square pan, which has been greased on the bottom only. Sprinkle with Topping. Bake at 350° for 45 to 50 minutes until cake springs back when touched lightly in center. Just before cake is done, prepare Sauce. Pour over warm cake. Cool before serving.

Topping: Combine all ingredients.

Sauce: In small saucepan, melt butter. Blend in remaining ingredients.

*For use with Pillsbury's Best Self-Rising Flour, omit salt and decrease soda to ¼ teaspoon.

Between the macaroon topping and the cake-like base is tucked a layer of strawberry preserves. Top with cream for dessert; or serve in bars.

Strawberry Blondes

1½ cups Pillsbury's Best All Purpose Flour*
½ cup sugar
1 teaspoon baking powder
¼ teaspoon salt
½ cup butter or margarine, softened
1 tablespoon water
¼ teaspoon almond extract
2 eggs
1 jar (10 oz.) or 1 cup strawberry preserves
1 package Pillsbury Fluffy White Frosting Mix
1 tablespoon butter or margarine, melted
1½ cups flaked coconut

OVEN 350°   12 SERVINGS

In large mixer bowl, combine flour, sugar, baking powder, salt, butter, water, almond extract and eggs. Blend well at low speed. Spread batter in greased and floured 13x9-inch pan. Top with preserves, spreading carefully to cover. Prepare frosting mix as directed on package. Fold in melted butter and coconut. Spread over preserves. Bake at 350° for 30 to 35 minutes or until light brown. Cool. Cut into bars or squares.

Tip: If desired, other flavors of preserves may be substituted.

*For use with Pillsbury's Best Self-Rising Flour, omit baking powder and salt.

Warm wedges of this savory apple-y cake are sure to be a hit. Served in wedges like pie but it's quick and easy apple cake.

Apple Pie-Cake

¼ cup butter or margarine
¾ cup sugar
1 egg
1 cup Pillsbury's Best All Purpose Flour*
1 teaspoon soda
1 teaspoon cinnamon
½ teaspoon salt
½ teaspoon nutmeg
⅛ teaspoon cloves
1 teaspoon vanilla

2 cups chopped apples
½ cup chopped nuts

OVEN 350°   5 TO 6 SERVINGS

In 3-quart saucepan, melt butter over medium heat. Remove from heat. Blend in sugar and egg. Add remaining ingredients; mix until blended. Turn into greased and floured 9 or 10-inch pie pan. Bake at 350° for 40 to 45 minutes or until top springs back when touched lightly. Serve warm or cold, cut in wedges, topped with whipped cream or ice cream.

*For use with Pillsbury's Best Self-Rising Flour, omit soda and salt.

Luscious cake squares chock full of cherries and nuts are topped with a sparkling red cherry sauce. An hour and fifteen minutes.

Saucy Cherry Squares

1 cup Pillsbury's Best All Purpose Flour*
1 cup sugar
1 teaspoon baking powder
½ teaspoon salt
1 tablespoon shortening
2 eggs
½ cup chopped walnuts
1 can (1 lb.) sour pie cherries, drain and reserve juice

Cherry Sauce
⅓ cup sugar
1 tablespoon cornstarch

OVEN 350°   8 TO 10 SERVINGS

In small mixer bowl, combine flour, sugar, baking powder, salt, shortening and eggs. Beat at medium speed until well blended. Fold in nuts and 1 cup of cherries. Spread in 9-inch square pan, greased on the bottom only. Bake at 350° for 35 to 40 minutes until top springs back when touched lightly in center. Serve warm or cold with warm Cherry Sauce and whipped cream or ice cream, if desired.

Cherry Sauce: In small saucepan, combine sugar, cornstarch, the reserved juice and remaining cherries. Cook over medium heat, stirring occasionally, until thick and clear. If desired, add 2 to 4 drops red food coloring.

*For use with Pillsbury's Best Self-Rising Flour, omit baking powder and salt.

A tropically moist pineapple cake under a topping of brown sugar and coconut. Comes to the luau warm or cold with whipped cream or ice cream.

Easy Hawaiian Torte

1½ cups Pillsbury's Best All Purpose Flour*
1 cup sugar
1 teaspoon soda
1 teaspoon salt
½ cup butter or margarine, softened
1 can (8½ oz.) or 1 cup crushed pineapple, undrained
1 teaspoon vanilla
1 egg
½ cup flaked coconut
½ cup firmly packed brown sugar

OVEN 350°   9 SERVINGS

In large mixer bowl, blend all ingredients, except coconut and brown sugar, at low speed. Beat 3 minutes at medium speed. Pour batter into greased and floured 9-inch square pan. Sprinkle with coconut and brown sugar. Bake at 350° for 35 to 40 minutes or until cake springs back when touched lightly in center. Serve warm or cold with whipped cream or ice cream.
*For use with Pillsbury's Best Self-Rising Flour, omit soda and salt.
HIGH ALTITUDE ADJUSTMENT — 5,200 FEET. Reduce soda to ½ teaspoon.

Gooey goodness in a one-step recipe. Pecans make it crunchy, fruit cocktail makes it moist. Ready in less than an hour.

Tuti Fruti Pudding

1 cup Pillsbury's Best All Purpose Flour*
1 cup sugar
1 teaspoon soda
½ teaspoon salt
1 can (1 lb.) fruit cocktail, drain and reserve ½ cup syrup
1 egg
¾ cup chopped pecans
½ cup firmly packed brown sugar

OVEN 350°   8 TO 10 SERVINGS

In small mixer bowl, blend all ingredients, except pecans and brown sugar, at lowest speed until thoroughly mixed. Spread batter evenly in bottom of greased and floured 9-inch square pan. Sprinkle with pecans and brown

sugar. Bake at 350° for 40 to 45 minutes until cake springs back when touched lightly. Serve warm with whipped cream or ice cream.
*For use with Pillsbury's Best Self-Rising Flour, increase flour to 1¼ cups, decrease soda to ¼ teaspoon and omit salt.
HIGH ALTITUDE ADJUSTMENT — 5,200 FEET. Reduce soda to ½ teaspoon.

The blender does the grinding and chopping for this orange-nut-date cake, moistened with orange juice and topped with whipped cream.

Orange Grove Dessert

2 eggs
1 cup sugar
⅔ cup dairy sour cream
⅓ cup shortening
1 medium orange, unpeeled, quartered, and seeds removed
1 cup dates
½ cup walnuts or pecans
2 cups Pillsbury's Best All Purpose Flour*
1½ teaspoons baking powder
½ teaspoon salt
½ teaspoon soda
½ cup sugar
½ cup orange juice

OVEN 350°   9-INCH CAKE

In blender container, put eggs, sugar, sour cream, shortening and orange. Cover and process at "blend" or medium speed until smooth. Add dates and walnuts; process at "blend" or medium speed for 2 cycles or about 5 seconds, just until dates and nuts have passed through blades. Pour into large mixing bowl. Add flour, baking powder, salt and soda; stir until well blended. Pour into greased and floured 9-inch square pan. Bake at 350° for 40 to 45 minutes until top springs back when touched lightly in center. Five minutes before cake is done, heat sugar and orange juice to boiling. Make holes in hot baked cake by piercing with toothpick. Pour hot orange juice mixture over, allowing to soak into cake. Serve warm or cold, topped with whipped cream.
*For use with Pillsbury's Best Self-Rising Flour, omit baking powder, soda and salt.
HIGH ALTITUDE ADJUSTMENT — 5,200 FEET. Reduce baking powder to 1 teaspoon, soda to ¼ teaspoon.

60

Pies, Pies And More Pies

● Here is a pie-lover's gallery of great ideas —
new combination fruit pies, many with unusual
toppings; custard pies rich with egg, pumpkin
or pecan-type fillings; a wide spectrum of fillings hidden under marvelous meringues, plus
a group of chilly favorites that are to be refrigerated just one or two hours before serving.
Let your eyes wander through and pick a perfect pie for any occasion.

Pies and Pastries

● Pies are always popular and with the products available today, they need not be difficult to make. Making good pie crust does take practice. There are many methods of making pastry and one will be just right for you. It may be one of the home recipe pastries, or perhaps you'll prefer the mix or sticks. We've included several ways here — maybe one of these will be best for you; maybe you have another you prefer. Perhaps our pastry hints will help . . . we strongly recommend the use of a cloth covered board and rolling pin. It makes rolling much, much easier.

Maybe you like to buy your pastry already prepared in the frozen food case or in the bakery. These work very nicely for one-crust pies. If you want to make a two-crust pie, try the streusel topping here or one of the variations in the Pies, Pies and More Pies chapter. They're tasty and pretty and never need rolling. One thing to remember in using these already prepared crusts is that most are in pans slightly smaller than regular 8 or 9-inch pie pans. Also, they do not have the high fluted edge. So, many times you'll have filling left over. Just pour the leftover into a small dish. Chill if the pie is chilled, or if the filling is baked, pour extra into an oven-proof dish and bake alongside pie. Because it is a smaller amount, it won't take as long to bake. These "extras" are great for after school or before bed snacks.

Pastry

Single Crust	Double Crust
1 cup Pillsbury's Best All Purpose Flour*	2 cups Pillsbury's Best All Purpose Flour*
½ teaspoon salt	1 teaspoon salt
⅓ cup shortening	⅔ cup shortening
3 to 4 tablespoons cold water	5 to 7 tablespoons cold water

In mixing bowl, combine flour and salt. Cut in shortening using a pastry blender or two knives until mixture is the size of small peas. Sprinkle water over mixture, a tablespoon at a time, while tossing and stirring lightly with fork. Add water until dough is just moist enough to hold together. (If there's too much water, it will be sticky and tough; if there's too little water, the edges will crack, the pastry will tear easily and it will be hard to roll out.) Form into a ball (2 balls for a double crust). Flatten each to ½-inch thickness on floured surface; smooth edges. Roll out to a circle 1 inch larger than inverted 8 or 9-inch pie pan. Fold pastry in half, transfer to pie pan, unfold and fit loosely into pan, gently patting out any air pockets.

*For use with Pillsbury's Best Self-Rising Flour, omit salt.

Unbaked Pastry Shell

Prepare Single Crust as directed on preceding page. Fold edges to form a standing rim; flute. Pour in filling and bake as directed in recipe.

Baked Pastry Shell

Prepare as directed for Unbaked Pastry Shell. Prick bottom and sides generously with fork. Bake at 450° for 8 to 10 minutes until light golden brown. Cool.

Double Crust Pastry

Prepare Double Crust as directed on preceding page, trimming bottom crust even with edge of pan. Pour filling into bottom crust. Roll out top crust; cut slits for escape of steam. Place top crust over filling. Fold top crust under bottom crust. Seal; flute edge.

Lattice Crust

Prepare pastry for double crust pie, leaving ½ inch extending beyond edge of pan. Roll out remainder of dough. Cut strips ½ inch wide (for pretty edge, use pastry wheel). Lay strips across filling in parallel rows about 1 inch apart, twisting if desired. Trim ends even with edge of pastry. Fold extension up over strips to form standing rim; flute.

Baked Pastry Tart Shells

For easy shells to hold pudding, ice cream or thickened fruit, prepare double crust pastry. Divide into 10 parts. Roll out each to a 4 to 5-inch round. Turn muffin pan upside down (or turn custard cups upside down on cookie sheet). Fit pastry circles over cup, pleating sides so pastry fits cup. Prick generously with fork. Bake at 450° for 8 to 10 minutes until golden brown. Cool. Remove from cups. Fill as desired.

Pie Crust Mix and Sticks

Pillsbury Pie Crust Mix or Sticks may be used for single or double crust. Prepare as directed on package. One package of mix makes enough for double crust; sticks come in 2 and 4 stick packages — one stick makes one single crust.

Cheese Pastry

Add shredded Cheddar or American cheese to flour or to pie crust mix or sticks. Use ½ cup for single crust; 1 cup for double crust.

Chocolate Pastry Shell

Add 3 tablespoons sugar, 3 tablespoons cocoa and ¼ teaspoon vanilla to single crust recipe. Prepare as directed for baked pastry shell, reducing temperature to 400°.

Vinegar Pastry

Some people like the extra flakiness that vinegar adds to pastry. Add 1 teaspoon sugar and 1 teaspoon vinegar for single crust. Prepare as directed.

Pastry Hints

Sprinkle water over mixture, a tablespoon at a time, while tossing and stirring. If water is added too fast, there will be wet spots in pastry that will be sure to stick when rolling out.

When making pie shells, be sure to ease pastry into pan. As it bakes, it shrinks slightly. If it has been stretched, it will shrink down into pan.

Flatten each ball to ½ inch thickness; smooth edges. By smoothing edges before rolling you prevent the cracked broken edges. If they start to crack, press together and smooth out — they just get bigger if you keep rolling.

To help keep sides on pastry shells, hook edge of fluted pastry over side of pan. This little "hook" helps hold it up on pie pan rim.

Roll out on floured surface. A cloth covered surface and a stockinette covered rolling pin are best. The flour goes further by being rubbed into the woven cloth and then used a little at a time, thus there is much less chance of pastry sticking or of too much flour on pastry.

Lattice crusts are easy and special made this way. Twist each strip as you place it on pie. It looks like you spent hours interweaving.

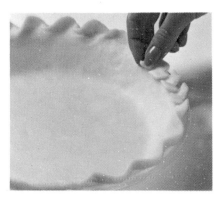

Add a special touch to your pie by fluting. First make edge stand up, then try one of these fluted edges. Makes pie as pretty as a picture.

Tips: With leftover pastry, make cut-outs and bake separately until golden brown, about 10 minutes. Place on top of 1 crust pies for decorative finish.

For an attractive shiny top crust, try brushing with milk or slightly beaten egg white. Sprinkle with sugar for a special glaze.

Streusel Topping

(Delicious on fruit pies — there's no top crust to roll out!)

> 1 cup Pillsbury's Best All Purpose or Self-Rising Flour
> ½ cup firmly packed brown sugar
> ½ teaspoon cinnamon
> ½ cup butter or margarine
> ¼ cup chopped nuts or flaked coconut, if desired

In mixing bowl, combine flour, brown sugar and cinnamon. Cut in butter until crumbly. Stir in nuts or coconut. Sprinkle over fruit filling. Bake as directed in recipe.

Meringue (3 egg white)

> 3 egg whites
> ¼ teaspoon cream of tartar
> ⅛ teaspoon salt
> ⅓ cup sugar

In small mixer bowl, beat egg whites with cream of tartar and salt at high speed until soft peaks form. Add sugar gradually. Continue beating until meringue stands in stiff peaks. Spoon meringue around edge of pie; seal to crust and then spread toward center, sealing in filling. Make swirls with back of teaspoon. Bake at 350° for 12 to 15 minutes or as directed in recipe.

Cookie Crumb Crusts

Cookie crumb crusts are easy because there's no rolling. These add a special crunchy goodness to pie fillings that are chilled and set up firm — gelatin or frozen fillings are best. Pick a cookie flavor that will enhance the flavor of your filling.

	Amount	Sugar	Butter or Margarine, melted
Graham cracker (crushed)	1½ Cups	¼ Cup	⅓ Cup
Vanilla wafers (crushed)	1½ Cups	Omit	¼ Cup
Gingersnaps (crushed)	1½ Cups	Omit	⅓ Cup
Cornflakes (crushed)	1½ Cups	¼ Cup	⅓ Cup
Chocolate creme-filled cookies (crushed)	2½ Cups	Omit	¼ Cup

Combine crumbs, sugar and melted butter until well mixed. Press into bottom and up sides of 9-inch pie pan. Bake at 375° for 8 to 10 minutes until golden brown. Cool.

Tip: The graham cracker, vanilla wafer, gingersnap and chocolate cookie crusts may be chilled without baking, if desired.

Refrigerated Cookie Crust

Slice about half a roll of Pillsbury Refrigerated Cookies ⅛ inch thick. Line bottom and sides of greased and lightly sugared pie pan, overlapping slightly. Bake at 375° for 8 to 10 minutes until golden brown. Cool. Fill with desired filling. Select a cookie flavor that goes with the filling.

Fruit Pies

Apple pie made special with cheesy pastry below and a spicy, crispy topping. Delightful served warm with cream cheese topping.

Cheesy Apple Crisp Pie

<u>9-inch unbaked Cheese Pastry Shell</u>, see page 63

    ½ cup sugar
    ⅓ cup firmly packed brown sugar
    2 tablespoons flour
    1 teaspoon ground coriander, if desired
    4 cups (4 medium) peeled, sliced apples
    ½ cup Pillsbury's Best All Purpose Flour*
    ⅓ cup sugar
    1 teaspoon grated lemon peel
    ½ teaspoon baking powder
    ½ teaspoon cinnamon
    ¼ teaspoon nutmeg
    ⅛ teaspoon salt
    ¼ cup butter or margarine, melted
    1 egg
    1 tablespoon milk

<u>Cheese Topping</u>

    1 package (3 oz.) cream cheese, softened
    1 tablespoon powdered sugar
    2 teaspoons lemon juice
    2 tablespoons sour cream

OVEN 375°   9-INCH PIE

In large mixing bowl, combine sugars, flour and coriander. Add apples and toss until apple slices are coated. Arrange in pastry-lined 9-inch pie pan. In small mixing bowl, combine ½ cup flour, ⅓ cup sugar, lemon peel, baking powder, cinnamon, nutmeg, salt, melted butter, egg and milk. Mix until well blended. Spread mixture over apples. Bake at 375° for 45 to 50 minutes, until apples are tender. Serve warm with Cheese Topping, if desired.

<u>Cheese Topping</u>: In small mixing bowl, combine all ingredients; blend until smooth. Chill until ready to use.

*For use with Pillsbury's Best Self-Rising Flour, omit baking powder and salt in crumb topping.

Red as an apple on a tree! You melt cinnamon candy to give new look, picture pretty through a lattice-top.

Red Cinnamon Apple Pie

<u>Double Crust Pastry</u>, Page 62

    ¾ cup sugar
    ½ cup water
    ¼ cup red cinnamon candies
    5 cups (5 medium) peeled, sliced apples
    3 tablespoons flour

OVEN 375°   9-INCH PIE

In saucepan, combine sugar, water and cinnamon candies. Simmer until candies are dissolved. Add apples and flour and cook until mixture is thickened. Pour into pastry-lined 9-inch pie pan. Roll out remaining dough, cut into strips ¾-inch wide and crisscross over filling to form lattice top. Trim and seal ends; fold bottom crust over to cover. Flute edge. Bake at 375° for 40 to 45 minutes, until golden brown and bubbly.

<u>Tips</u>: Prepared apple pie filling may be used. Combine with red cinnamon candies and cook over medium heat until candies are dissolved. Pour into pastry-lined pan.

For help in making lattice crust, see page 63.

Red Cinnamon Apple Pie

Apricot Crunch Pie

Apricots and dates make the perfect filling for the simple crunchy topping. Easy to make and the family will love it.

Apricot Crunch Pie

9-inch Unbaked Pastry Shell, see page 63

    I can (1 lb. 14 oz.) unpeeled apricot halves, drain and reserve ½ cup syrup

    I cup chopped dates

    ¼ cup sugar

    2 tablespoons quick-cooking tapioca

    I teaspoon grated lemon peel

    2 tablespoons lemon juice

    ½ teaspoon cinnamon

Topping

    ½ cup quick-cooking rolled oats

    ½ cup firmly packed brown sugar

    ⅓ cup Pillsbury's Best All Purpose or Self-Rising Flour

    ⅓ cup butter or margarine, melted

OVEN 400°   9-INCH PIE

Cut apricots in half; arrange in unbaked pastry shell along with dates. In mixing bowl, combine sugar, tapioca, lemon peel, lemon juice, cinnamon and reserved syrup; pour over fruit. Sprinkle with Topping. Bake at 400° for 45 to 50 minutes until golden brown and bubbly.

Topping: In mixing bowl, combine all ingredients; mix well.

In the fall, gather apricots and raisins and bake them in a pretty lattice-crust topped pie. Prepared pie filling makes it simple.

Autumn Glory Pie

Orange Pastry

    1½ cups Pillsbury's Best All Purpose Flour*

    ¾ teaspoon salt

    ½ cup shortening

    I tablespoon grated orange peel

    3 tablespoons orange juice

    2 tablespoons water

Apricot-Raising Filling

    I can (I lb. 5 oz.) prepared apricot pie filling

    I cup raisins

    2 teaspoons grated lemon peel, *if desired*

OVEN 400°   8-INCH PIE

Orange Pastry: In small mixing bowl, combine flour and salt. Cut in shortening until particles are the size of small peas. Combine orange peel, juice and water; sprinkle over dry ingredients while tossing and stirring lightly with fork. Add to driest particles, pushing lumps to side, until dough is just moist enough to hold together. Divide into two parts, one twice as large as the other. Form into balls. Flatten to about ½-inch thickness; smooth edges. Roll out larger portion on floured surface to a circle 1½ inches larger than inverted 8-inch pie pan. Fit loosely into pan. Spread Apricot-Raisin Filling in pastry-lined pan. Roll out remaining dough. Cut into strips ½ inch wide; crisscross over filling to form a lattice top. Trim and seal ends. Fold bottom crust over to cover; flute. Bake at 400° for 20 to 25 minutes until golden brown.

Apricot-Raisin Filling: In small mixing bowl, combine all ingredients.

Tips: For plain pastry, omit orange peel and use all water for liquid.

For help in making lattice crust, see page 63.

*For use with Pillsbury's Best Self-Rising Flour, omit salt in Orange Pastry.

Picture-pretty pie with pastry cut-out top . . . inside a rich apple-butter and cheese filling. Ummmm.

Apple-Scotch Cheese Pie

Pastry
   1½ cups Pillsbury's Best All Purpose Flour*
   ½ teaspoon salt
   ⅔ cup shortening
   4 to 5 tablespoons cold water

Apple-Cheese Filling
   1 cup sugar
   1 cup apple butter
   ¾ cup shredded process American cheese
   ¼ cup Pillsbury's Best All Purpose Flour
   ¼ cup butter or margarine, softened
   ¼ teaspoon salt
   3 eggs

OVEN 375°   9-INCH PIE

Pastry: In large mixing bowl, combine flour and salt. Cut in shortening until mixture is the size of small peas. Sprinkle water over mixture, a little at a time, tossing and stirring lightly with fork. Form into a ball. Roll out two-thirds of dough, on floured surface, 1½ inches larger than inverted 9-inch pie pan. Fit loosely in pan. Flute edge. Pour Apple-Cheese Filling into pastry-lined pan. Roll out remaining pastry and cut into six triangles with cookie cutter. Place on ungreased cookie sheet. Bake pie at 375° for 40 to 45 minutes until golden brown. Bake pastry cutouts at 375° for 10 to 12 minutes. Cool pie; arrange cutouts on filling.

Apple-Cheese Filling: In small mixer bowl, combine filling ingredients. Mix at low speed until well blended.

Tip: Or, use 9-inch unbaked pastry shell. Omit pastry cutouts.

For use with Pillsbury's Best Self-Rising Flour, omit salt in Pastry.

Pineapple Crunch Pie

Sweet pineapple meets crunchy pecan glazed crust for a great new duo in pies. A refreshing, interesting new flavor.

Pineapple Crunch Pie

Double Crust Pastry, see page 62
   2 tablespoons sugar
   2 tablespoons cornstarch
   ¼ teaspoon salt
   1 can (1 lb. 4½ oz.) crushed pineapple, undrained
   1 tablespoon butter or margarine
   1 tablespoon lemon juice

Topping
   ¼ cup firmly packed brown sugar
   2 tablespoons butter or margarine
   1 tablespoon cornstarch
   1 tablespoon water
   ½ cup chopped pecans

OVEN 425°   8-INCH PIE

In saucepan, combine sugar, cornstarch, salt and pineapple. Cook over medium heat, stirring occasionally, until thick. Add butter and lemon juice; blend well. Pour into pastry-lined 8-inch pie pan. Roll out remaining dough. Cut slits for escape of steam. Moisten rim of bottom crust. Place top crust over filling. Fold edge under bottom crust, pressing to seal; flute edge. Spread warm Topping over crust. Bake at 425° for 25 to 30 minutes until deep golden brown.

Topping: In small saucepan, combine all ingredients except pecans. Cook over low heat, stirring occasionally, until sugar is dissolved. Add pecans.

Sweet and slightly sassy rhubarb custard peeps through the criss-cross pastry top. Easy does it, too!

Creamy Rhubarb Pie

Double Crust Pastry, see page 62

      2 eggs
   1½ cups sugar
      2 tablespoons flour
   ½ teaspoon salt
      1 tablespoon soft butter or margarine
      2 packages (1 lb. each) frozen rhubarb, thawed and drained

OVEN 375°   9-INCH PIE

In large mixing bowl, combine eggs, sugar, flour, salt and soft butter. Mix until well blended. Stir in rhubarb. Pour into pastry-lined 9-inch pie pan. Roll out remaining dough. Cut into strips ½-inch wide; crisscross over filling to form lattice top. Fold edge under bottom crust, pressing to seal. Flute edge. Bake at 375° for 40 to 45 minutes until golden brown and bubbly. Cool.

Tips: *4 cups fresh cut-up rhubarb may be used in place of frozen rhubarb.*

For sweeter pie, use 2 cups sugar.

It's like old-fashioned apple pie with cinnamon . . . only better because there is pineapple added.

Pine-Apple Pie

Double Crust Pastry, see page 62

      4 cups (4 medium) peeled, sliced apples
      1 can (8½ oz.) or 1 cup crushed pineapple, undrained
   ⅔ cup sugar
      3 tablespoons flour
      1 teaspoon cinnamon

OVEN 375°   9-INCH PIE

In mixing bowl, combine apples, pineapple, sugar, flour and cinnamon. Pour into pastry-lined 9-inch pie pan. Roll out remaining dough; cut slits for steam to escape. Moisten rim of bottom crust. Place top crust over apple mixture. Fold edge under bottom crust, pressing to seal. Flute edge. Bake at 375° for 45 to 50 minutes, until apples are tender.

Tip: *1 can prepared apple pie filling may be used; omit sugar and flour.*

Nothing like Grandma's . . . we've changed the shape and added the zing of rich caramel nut flavor to good, old apple pie. It's mod!

Apple Pie '63

      1 package Pillsbury Pie Crust Mix or Sticks
      3 cups (about 3 medium) peeled, sliced apples
   ½ cup sugar
      2 tablespoons flour
      1 tablespoon lemon juice
   ¼ cup caramel ice cream topping
   ¼ cup chopped walnuts

Topping
      2 tablespoons sugar
      1 package (3 oz.) cream cheese, softened
      1 egg

OVEN 375°   8 TO 10 SERVINGS

Prepare pie crust mix as directed on package for double crust pie. Roll out dough on floured surface to a 14-inch circle. Place on cookie sheet; form rim. In mixing bowl, combine apples, sugar, flour and lemon juice; mix well. Arrange on crust; drizzle with ice cream topping. Spoon Topping between ice cream topping; sprinkle with nuts. Bake at 375° for 30 to 35 minutes until lightly browned. Serve warm or cold.

Topping: In mixer bowl, combine all ingredients at high speed until smooth and fluffy.

Exotic butter-crumb topping on peach-raspberry filling. It just tastes like it was hard to make. It isn't!

Melba Streusel Pie

9-inch Unbaked Pastry Shell, see page 63

Filling

>   ¼ cup sugar
>   3 tablespoons cornstarch
>   ¼ teaspoon cinnamon
>   I tablespoon lemon juice
>   I can (I lb. 13 oz.) peach slices, drained
>   I package (10 oz.) frozen raspberries,
>   thawed and drained

Topping

>   ¾ cup Pillsbury's Best All Purpose or
>   Self-Rising Flour
>   ½ cup firmly packed brown sugar
>   ¼ cup butter or margarine

OVEN 375°   9-INCH PIE

Filling: In large mixing bowl, combine sugar, cornstarch, cinnamon and lemon juice. Stir in peaches and raspberries. Turn into unbaked pastry shell. Sprinkle on Topping. Bake at 375° for 30 to 35 minutes until golden brown and bubbly. Cool.

Topping: In small mixing bowl, combine flour and brown sugar. Cut in butter until mixture is crumbly.

Fresh from the Islands, the cool gold and white of tangy fresh pineapple and snowwhite coconut in a double crust.

Waikiki Pie

Double Crust Pastry, see page 62

>   I egg, beaten
>   I cup grated coconut
>   I cup sugar
>   I tablespoon flour
>   2 cups cut-up fresh pineapple

OVEN 400°   9-INCH PIE

In large mixing bowl, combine egg, coconut, sugar and flour; stir in pineapple. Pour into pastry-lined 9-inch pie pan. Roll out remaining dough. Cut slits for escape of steam. Moisten rim of bottom crust. Place top crust over

filling. Fold edge under bottom crust, pressing to seal; flute edge. Bake at 400° for 35 to 40 minutes until golden brown and bubbly. Cool.

Tips: 2 cans (13¼ oz. each) pineapple chunks, drained, or 2 cans (13¼ oz. each) frozen pineapple chunks, thawed and drained, may be substituted for fresh pineapple.

If desired, I large banana, sliced, and ½ teaspoon orange extract may be added with the pineapple.

Brown sugar caramel and nuts baked on the bottom of a two crust apple pie, turned upside down to serve.

Topsy Turvy Apple Pie

Double Crust Pastry, see below

>   ¼ cup firmly packed brown sugar
>   1½ tablespoons butter or margarine, melted
>   I tablespoon corn syrup
>   ¼ cup pecan halves
>   ⅔ cup sugar
>   2 tablespoons flour
>   ½ teaspoon cinnamon
>   4 cups (4 medium) peeled, sliced apples

OVEN 375°   9-INCH PIE

In 9-inch pie pan, combine brown sugar, melted butter and corn syrup. Arrange pecan halves on top. Prepare Double Crust Pastry, see page 62, adding ¼ teaspoon cinnamon to flour mixture. Roll out half of pastry on floured surface 1½ inches larger than inverted 9-inch pie pan. Fit loosely over sugar-pecan mixture. In small mixing bowl, combine sugar, flour and cinnamon. Arrange sliced apples in layers, sprinkling sugar mixture over each layer. Roll out remaining dough; cut slits for steam to escape. Moisten rim of bottom crust. Place top crust over apple mixture. Fold edge under bottom crust, pressing to seal. Flute edge. Bake at 375° for 45 to 50 minutes, until apples are tender. Loosen edge of pie; then invert on serving plate, bottom-side up.

Tip: I can prepared apple pie filling may be used in place of apple filling.

Start with prepared apple pie filling but give this pie an easy topper! A chewy topping full of coconut.

Coconut Crunch Apple Pie

9-inch Unbaked Pastry Shell, see page 63

    I can (1 lb. 5 oz.) prepared apple pie filling
    I egg
    1/3 cup sugar
    1/4 cup milk
    1/8 teaspoon salt
    2 cups flaked coconut

OVEN 375°   9-INCH PIE

Pour pie filling into unbaked pastry shell. In small mixer bowl, combine egg, sugar, milk and salt. Mix at low speed until well blended. Stir in coconut; mix well. Spread over apple filling. Bake at 375° for 25 to 30 minutes until golden brown.

Ooh-la-la! A layer of spiced apples covered with a refreshing cream cheese sauce, all hidden between a golden crust. The family will love it; company too.

French Apple Creme Pie

Double Crust Pastry, see page 62

    I can (1 lb. 5 oz.) prepared apple pie filling
    I teaspoon grated lemon peel
    1/4 teaspoon cinnamon
    1/4 teaspoon nutmeg
    I package (3 oz.) cream cheese, softened
    1/3 cup sugar
    1/4 cup dairy sour cream
    I tablespoon lemon juice
    I egg

OVEN 425°   9-INCH PIE

In small mixing bowl, combine pie filling, lemon peel, cinnamon and nutmeg. Pour into pastry-lined 9-inch pie pan. In small mixing bowl, combine remaining ingredients; beat until smooth and creamy. Pour over apple mixture. Roll out remaining dough; cut slits for steam to escape. Moisten rim of bottom crust. Place top crust over filling. Fold edge under bottom crust, pressing to seal. Flute edge. Bake at 425° for 25 to 30 minutes until golden brown. Cool completely.

Spicy crumb crust makes this pear pie extra crunchy good for guests or family. Make it fast with pie crust mix or sticks.

Pear Crunch Pie

Pastry Shell and Filling

    I package Pillsbury Pie Crust Sticks
    2 tablespoons sugar
    1 1/2 tablespoons cornstarch
    Dash salt
    Dash nutmeg
    I can (1 lb. 13 oz.) pear halves, drain and reserve 1 cup syrup
    1/2 teaspoon grated lemon peel
    2 teaspoons lemon juice
    I tablespoon butter or margarine

Crumb Topping

    1/2 cup firmly packed brown sugar
    1/2 cup chopped walnuts
    1/4 teaspoon cinnamon
    1/4 teaspoon nutmeg

OVEN 425°   9-INCH PIE

Shell and Filling: Prepare one pie crust stick as directed on package for 9-inch unbaked pastry shell. In saucepan, combine sugar, cornstarch, salt and nutmeg; gradually add reserved pear syrup, mix well. Cook over medium heat, stirring occasionally, until thick. Add lemon peel, lemon juice and butter; blend well. Cut pears in half; arrange in pastry-lined pan. Cover with thickened pear syrup. Sprinkle with Crumb Topping. Bake at 425° for 20 to 25 minutes until golden brown. Serve warm with whipped cream.

Crumb Topping: In small mixing bowl, crumble remaining pie crust stick. Add brown sugar, walnuts, cinnamon and nutmeg; mix well.

Tip: Pillsbury Pie Crust Mix may be substituted for pie crust sticks. Prepare 9-inch unbaked pastry shell as directed on package. Combine remaining mix with brown sugar, nuts and spices for topping.

As convenient as opening cans . . . with pre-pared mincemeat and peach pie filling in a two-crust pie. Quick to do in an hour and a quarter.

Mincey Peach Pie

<u>Double Crust Pastry</u>, see page 62

  1½ cups prepared mincemeat
    1 can (1 lb. 5 oz.) prepared peach pie filling
    2 teaspoons grated orange peel
     Cream
     Sugar, if desired

OVEN 375°   9-INCH PIE

In large mixing bowl, combine mincemeat, pie filling and orange peel. Pour into pastry-lined 9-inch pie pan. Roll out remaining dough; cut slits for steam to escape. Moisten rim of bottom crust. Place top crust over filling. Fold edge under bottom crust, pressing to seal. Flute edge. Brush top crust with cream; sprinkle with sugar, if desired. Bake at 375° for 40 to 45 minutes until golden brown.

Mincey Peach Pie

The duchess of strawberry pies. Pretty straw-berries peeking through the golden lattice crust.

Strawberry Pie
Delicious

Strawberry Pie Delicious

<u>Double Crust Pastry</u>, see page 62

    4 packages (10 oz. each) frozen strawberry
      halves, drain and reserve ¼ cup syrup
  ½ cup drained pineapple tidbits
  3 tablespoons cornstarch
  2 tablespoons sugar
  ½ teaspoon salt
    Milk

OVEN 400°   9-INCH PIE

In mixing bowl, combine strawberries, re-served juice, pineapple, cornstarch, sugar and salt; blend well. Pour into pastry-lined 9-inch pie pan. Roll out remaining dough. Cut into strips ½ inch wide; crisscross over filling to form lattice top. Trim and seal ends; fold bottom crust over to cover. Flute. Brush strips with milk. Bake at 400° for 35 to 40 minutes or until crust is golden brown.

<u>Tip:</u> See page 63 for help in making a lattice crust.

73

Thin slices of tart lemon smothered in a creamy custard filling and baked in flaky pastry. A refreshing finish to any meal.

Two-Crust Slice O' Lemon Pie

Double Crust Pastry, see page 62

Filling
- 1¼ cups sugar
- 2 tablespoons flour
- ⅛ teaspoon salt
- ½ cup water
- ¼ cup butter or margarine, melted
- 3 eggs
- 1 teaspoon grated lemon peel
- 1 lemon, peeled and sliced thin

OVEN 400°   8-INCH PIE

In small mixing bowl, combine all filling ingredients except peeled lemon slices. Mix until well blended. Stir in lemon slices. Pour into pastry-lined 8-inch pie pan. Roll out remaining dough. Cut slits for steam to escape; moisten rim of bottom crust. Place top crust over filling. Fold edge under bottom crust, pressing to seal. Flute edge. Bake at 400° for 30 to 35 minutes until golden brown. Chill before serving.

A great new mix of fall fruits! A two-crust pie filled with apples, cranberries and apricots. They're great go-togethers . . . a fall treat!

Harvest Moon Fruit Pie

Double Crust Pastry, see page 62

- 1½ cups sugar
- ¼ cup cornstarch
- ½ teaspoon cinnamon
- ¼ teaspoon salt
- ¼ teaspoon nutmeg
- 3 cups (3 medium) peeled and thinly sliced apples
- 1 cup fresh or frozen cranberries, ground
- 1 cup dried apricots, ground
- Milk
- Sugar

OVEN 375°   9-INCH PIE

In large mixing bowl, combine sugar, cornstarch, cinnamon, salt and nutmeg; stir in apples, cranberries and apricots. Turn into 9-inch pastry-lined pie pan. Roll out remaining dough; cut slits for escape of steam. Moisten rim of bottom crust. Place top crust over filling. Fold edge under bottom crust, pressing to seal. Flute edge. Brush top with milk; sprinkle with sugar. Bake at 375° for 45 to 50 minutes until golden brown. Serve warm.

Harvest Moon Fruit Pie

Start with pie shell, arrange pear halves in petals. Now cover with a currant glaze and chill. Beautiful!

Pink Petal Pie

Pastry

    1 cup Pillsbury's Best All Purpose or
       Self-Rising Flour
  1/4 cup sugar
  1/3 cup butter or margarine
    2 teaspoons grated lemon peel
    1 egg yolk

Filling

    1 can (1 lb. 13 oz.) pear halves, drain and
      reserve 1/2 cup syrup
    2 tablespoons cornstarch
    1 teaspoon grated lemon peel
    1 tablespoon lemon juice
  1/2 cup currant or apple jelly

OVEN 425°   9-INCH PIE

Pastry: In small mixing bowl, combine flour and sugar. Cut in butter until particles are fine. Stir in lemon peel. Add egg yolk and mix until well blended. Press into a 9-inch pie pan. Bake at 425° for 10 minutes. Cool.

Filling: Arrange pears, cut-side down petal-fashion in crust. In small saucepan, combine remaining ingredients with reserved pear syrup. Cook over medium heat, stirring constantly, until thick and clear. Spoon over pear halves. Chill several hours before serving. Garnish with whipped cream, if desired.

Tip: If desired, use a 9-inch baked pastry shell, page 63.

Peaches and cherries on a cheese crust! A truly original fruit pizza dessert that will have them guessing ingredients at the first bite. Serve warm or cold.

Peach Carousel

Crust and Filling

  1 1/2 cups Pillsbury's Best All Purpose Flour*
    1 package (4 oz.) or 1 cup shredded
      Cheddar cheese
    1 teaspoon salt
  1/2 cup shortening
    4 to 5 tablespoons water
  1/3 cup butterscotch ice cream topping
    1 can (1 lb. 13 oz.) or 2 cups peach slices,
      drained
    1 tablespoon lemon juice
  1/4 cup maraschino cherry halves

Crunchy Topping

  1/2 cup chopped pecans
  1/4 cup sugar
  1/4 cup firmly packed brown sugar
    1 tablespoon cornstarch
  1/2 teaspoon cinnamon
  1/2 teaspoon nutmeg

OVEN 425°   8 TO 10 SERVINGS

Crust and Filling: In large mixing bowl, combine flour, cheese and salt. Cut in shortening until particles are the size of small peas. Sprinkle water over mixture while tossing lightly with a fork until particles just hold together. Press onto bottom of 12-inch pizza pan forming a 1/2-inch standing rim; flute edge. Spread ice cream topping over pastry. Place peaches, petal fashion, on topping; sprinkle with lemon juice, then Crunchy Topping. Garnish with cherry halves. Bake at 425° for 25 to 30 minutes until crust is golden. Serve warm or cold cut in wedges and topped with whipped cream.

Crunchy Topping: Combine all ingredients in a small mixing bowl.

Tip: If you don't have a pizza pan, press out dough into a 12-inch circle on a cookie sheet, forming 1/2-inch standing rim.

*For use with Pillsbury's Best Self-Rising Flour, omit salt.

Bright cherry and strawberry filling with a crispy, crunchy streusel topping made with a mix. Simple to make in less than an hour.

Cherry-Berry Pie

Pastry Shell and Topping
>   I package Pillsbury Pie Crust Sticks
>   ¼ cup chopped walnuts
>   ¼ cup firmly packed brown sugar
>   ½ teaspoon cinnamon

Filling
>   I can (I lb. 5 oz.) prepared cherry pie
>   filling
>   I package (10 oz.) frozen strawberry halves,
>   thawed and drained
>   I tablespoon cornstarch
>   I tablespoon lemon juice

OVEN 425°   9-INCH PIE

Shell and Topping: Prepare one pie crust stick as directed on package for 9-inch unbaked pastry shell. Pour Filling into unbaked pastry shell. In mixing bowl, crumble remaining pie crust stick. Add walnuts, brown sugar and cinnamon; mix well. Sprinkle over Filling. Bake at 425° for 25 to 30 minutes or until brown and bubbly. Cool before serving.

Filling: Combine all ingredients in mixing bowl; mix well.

Tip: Pillsbury Pie Crust Mix may be substituted for pie crust sticks. Prepare 9-inch unbaked pastry shell as directed on package. Combine remaining mix with nuts, brown sugar and cinnamon for topping.

Snappy spices spark this apple and date layered delight. A surprise duet in a double crust.

Apple Date Pie

Double Crust Pastry, see page 62
>   ⅔ cup sugar
>   2 tablespoons flour
>   ½ teaspoon cinnamon
>   ¼ teaspoon salt
>   ¼ teaspoon nutmeg
>   ⅛ to ¼ teaspoon ginger
>   I teaspoon grated lemon peel
>   5 cups (5 medium) peeled, sliced apples
>   ½ cup cut-up dates
>   I teaspoon lemon juice
>   I tablespoon butter or margarine

OVEN 375°   9-INCH PIE

In small mixing bowl, combine sugar, flour, cinnamon, salt, nutmeg, ginger and lemon peel. Arrange apples and dates in layers in pastry-lined 9-inch pie pan, sprinkling each layer with sugar-spice mixture. Sprinkle on lemon juice; dot with butter. Roll out remaining dough; cut slits for steam to escape. Moisten rim of bottom crust. Place top crust over filling. Fold edge under bottom crust, pressing to seal. Flute edge. Bake at 375° for 45 to 50 minutes until golden brown and apples are tender. Serve warm.

Filling is a delicate blend of peaches and spices topped with lemony cheesecake layer.

Peacheesy Pie

9-inch Unbaked Pastry Shell, see page 63

Peach Filling
>   I can (I lb. 13 oz.) peach slices, drain and
>   reserve 2 tablespoons syrup
>   ½ cup sugar
>   2 tablespoons cornstarch
>   2 tablespoons light corn syrup
>   2 teaspoons pumpkin pie spice
>   2 teaspoons vanilla

Cheesecake Topping
>   2 eggs, slightly beaten
>   ⅓ cup sugar
>   2 tablespoons peach syrup
>   I tablespoon lemon juice
>   I package (3 oz.) cream cheese
>   ½ cup dairy sour cream

OVEN 375°   9-INCH PIE

Peach Filling: In large mixing bowl, combine all ingredients. Stir gently to blend. Pour into unbaked pastry shell. Pour Cheesecake Topping over peach mixture. Bake at 375° for 40 to 50 minutes until topping is set and crust is golden brown. Chill.

Cheesecake Topping: In small saucepan, combine eggs, sugar, syrup and lemon juice. Cook, stirring constantly, until thick. In small mixer bowl, beat cream cheese until soft. Blend in sour cream. Add hot mixture; beat until smooth.

In between two flaky layers of crust are all sorts of delicious fruits in an old-world favorite families love.

Scandinavian "Fruit Soup" Pie

Double Crust Pastry, see page 62

⅔ cup sugar
3 tablespoons cornstarch
⅛ teaspoon salt
¾ cup orange juice
½ cup prune juice
2 tablespoons lemon juice
¾ cup applesauce
½ cup currants
1 cup cooked prunes, cut up
1½ teaspoons grated orange peel
1 tablespoon butter or margarine
Milk
Sugar

OVEN 400°   9-INCH PIE

In saucepan, combine sugar, cornstarch and salt; stir in orange juice, prune juice and lemon juice. Cook over medium heat, stirring occasionally, until thick. Add applesauce, currants, prunes, orange peel and butter; mix well. Turn into pastry-lined 9-inch pie pan. Roll out remaining dough. Cut into strips ½-inch wide; crisscross over filling to form lattice top. Trim and seal ends; fold bottom crust over to cover. Flute. Brush strips with milk and sprinkle with sugar. Bake at 400° for 25 to 30 minutes until golden brown. Cool.

Beneath the elegant lattice top rests a feast of peaches and pineapple with just a slight spice of cinnamon.

Hawaiian Holiday Pie

Double Crust Pastry, see page 62

1 can (1 lb. 5 oz.) prepared peach pie filling
1 tablespoon cornstarch, if desired
1 teaspoon cinnamon
1 tablespoon lemon juice
1 can (8½ oz.) pineapple tidbits, drained
Milk
Sugar

OVEN 400°   8-INCH PIE

In mixing bowl, combine pie filling, cornstarch, cinnamon and lemon juice. Spread filling in 8-inch pastry-lined pie pan. Sprinkle with pineapple tidbits. Roll out remaining dough. Cut into strips ½-inch wide; crisscross over filling to form lattice top. Trim and seal ends; fold bottom crust over to cover. Flute. Brush strips with milk; sprinkle with sugar. Bake at 400° for 30 to 35 minutes until crust is golden brown.

Tip: If desired, top with plain top crust instead of lattice crust.

The new expression is . . . goes together like peaches and butterscotch. Pretty looking too with a criss-cross crust.

Peachy Scotch Pie

Double Crust Pastry, see page 62

⅔ cup firmly packed brown sugar
3 tablespoons flour
½ teaspoon salt
¼ cup butter or margarine
1 tablespoon lemon juice
¼ teaspoon vanilla or almond extract
1 can (1 lb. 13 oz.) or 2½ cups peach slices, drained

OVEN 400°   9-INCH PIE

In saucepan, combine brown sugar, flour, salt, butter, lemon juice and vanilla extract; mix well. Bring to rolling boil, over medium heat, stirring constantly. Boil 1 minute. Stir in peach slices. Pour into 9-inch pastry-lined pie pan. Roll out remaining dough. Cut into strips ½ inch wide; crisscross over filling to form a lattice top. Trim and seal ends. Fold bottom crust over to cover; flute. Bake at 400° for 40 to 45 minutes until crust is golden brown.

Tips: If fluted edge of crust becomes too brown, cover with a thin strip of foil.

See page 63 for help in making a lattice crust.

The flavor and aroma of spicy mincemeat, but it's apple . . . you'll just have to taste it to believe.

Frosty Mince Believe Pie

Double Crust Pastry, see page 62

   1 can (1 lb. 5 oz.) prepared apple pie filling
   1 cup raisins
   ¼ cup firmly packed brown sugar
   ½ teaspoon cinnamon
   ⅛ teaspoon cloves
   ¼ cup orange marmalade
   2 tablespoons butter or margarine, softened
   1 tablespoon lemon juice

OVEN 375°   9-INCH PIE

In large mixing bowl, combine all ingredients. Blend well. Pour into pastry-lined 9-inch pie pan. Roll out remaining dough; cut slits for steam to escape. Moisten rim of bottom crust. Place top crust over filling. Fold edge under bottom crust, pressing to seal. Flute edge. Bake at 375° for 35 to 40 minutes until golden brown. Serve warm.

Apples and cream make this mincemeat pie special with its freckled crust of chopped walnuts. A delicious and fun idea!

Orchard Mince Pie

9-inch Unbaked Pastry Shell, see page 63

   2 cups (2 to 3 medium) peeled and finely
      chopped apples
   1 cup prepared mincemeat
   ¾ cup light cream
   ¾ cup firmly packed brown sugar
   ¼ teaspoon salt
   ½ cup chopped walnuts

OVEN 375°   9-INCH PIE

In large mixing bowl, combine apples, mincemeat, cream, brown sugar and salt. Blend well. Pour into unbaked pastry shell; sprinkle with walnuts. Bake at 375° for 40 to 45 minutes until crust is golden brown.

One crust is pastry, the top is buttery crumble. Inside your old favorite—rhubarb—either fresh or frozen.

Rhubarb Crumble Pie

8-inch Unbaked Pastry Shell, see page 63

   2 tablespoons sugar
   2 tablespoons flour
   1 package (1 lb.) frozen rhubarb, thaw,
      drain and reserve syrup
   2 drops red food coloring

Topping
   ¾ cup Pillsbury's Best All Purpose Flour*
   ½ cup sugar
   ¼ teaspoon salt
   ¼ cup butter or margarine

OVEN 375°   8-INCH PIE

In saucepan, combine sugar and flour. Stir in reserved rhubarb syrup and red food coloring. Cook over medium heat, stirring constantly, until thick. Remove from heat; stir in rhubarb. Pour into unbaked pastry shell. Sprinkle on Topping. Bake at 375° for 35 to 40 minutes. Cool.

Topping: In small mixing bowl, combine flour, sugar and salt. Cut in butter until mixture is crumbly.

Tip: 3 cups fresh cut-up rhubarb may be used in filling. Mix with ¾ cup sugar and 2 tablespoons flour. Pour into pastry shell.

*For use with Pillsbury's Best Self-Rising Flour, omit salt in Topping.

78

Rhubarb Crumble Pie

A double crust treat! Juicy, sliced pears combine with the spices of apple pie for a succulent new flavor! Is it apple or is it pear?

Fresh Pear Pie

Double Crust Pastry, see page 62

   ½ cup sugar
   3 tablespoons flour
   1 teaspoon cinnamon
   ¼ teaspoon salt
   5 cups (5 or 6 medium) peeled and sliced
      pears
   1 tablespoon butter or margarine
   1 teaspoon grated lemon peel, if desired
   1 tablespoon lemon juice
      Milk
      Sugar

OVEN 400°   9-INCH PIE

In small mixing bowl, combine sugar, flour, cinnamon and salt. Arrange pear slices in layers in pastry-lined 9-inch pie pan, sprinkling sugar mixture over each layer. Dot with butter; sprinkle with lemon peel and lemon juice. Roll out remaining dough; cut slits for escape of steam. Moisten rim of bottom crust. Place top crust over filling. Fold edge under bottom crust, pressing to seal. Flute edge. Brush top with milk; sprinkle with sugar. Bake at 400° for 40 to 45 minutes until pears are tender.

Tip: 1 can (1 lb. 13 oz.) pear halves, drained and sliced, may be substituted for fresh pears. Reduce sugar to ¼ cup, flour to 2 tablespoons. Bake at 400° for 30 minutes until golden brown.

Rich, tasty mincemeat is set off by a tart, sponge topping. A refreshing touch to an old favorite.

Lemon-Topped Mince Pie

9-inch Unbaked Pastry Shell, see page 63

Mincemeat Filling
   2 cups prepared mincemeat
   ¼ cup walnuts, chopped

Lemon Topping
   ⅔ cup sugar
   2 tablespoons flour
   ¾ cup milk
   2 tablespoons butter or margarine,
      softened
   2 tablespoons lemon juice
   1 tablespoon grated lemon peel
   2 eggs, separated

OVEN 350°   9-INCH PIE

Mincemeat Filling: In small mixing bowl, combine mincemeat and walnuts. Pour into unbaked pastry shell. Spoon Lemon Topping carefully over mincemeat mixture. Bake at 350° for 45 to 50 minutes until golden brown.

Lemon Topping: In large mixer bowl, combine sugar, flour, milk, butter, lemon juice, lemon peel and egg yolks. Mix until well blended at low speed. Beat egg whites until soft peaks form; gently fold into lemon mixture.

A sour cream custard makes the perfect setting for gingered pear halves. All topped off with crunchy sugar 'n spice topping.

French Pear Pie

9-inch Unbaked Pastry Shell, see page 63
   1 can (1 lb. 13 oz.) pear halves, drained
   ⅓ cup sugar
   ⅛ teaspoon ginger
   1 cup dairy sour cream
   1 egg

Crumb Topping
   ½ cup Pillsbury's Best All Purpose Flour
   ¼ cup firmly packed brown sugar
   ½ teaspoon nutmeg
   ¼ cup butter or margarine

OVEN 400°   9-INCH PIE

Arrange pear halves, cut side up, in unbaked pastry shell. In small mixing bowl, combine sugar, ginger, sour cream and egg; mix until thoroughly blended. Pour over pears. Sprinkle with Crumb Topping. Bake at 400° for 25 to 30 minutes until golden brown. Cool.

Crumb Topping: In small mixing bowl, combine flour, brown sugar and nutmeg. Cut in butter until particles are fine.

Custard Pies

Old-fashioned sour cream custard, spicy and good . . . dappled all through with raisins. This is easy to bake.

Raisin Cream Smoothie Pie

9-inch Unbaked Pastry Shell, see page 63

      3 eggs
   1¼ cups sugar
      1 teaspoon cinnamon
    ½ teaspoon salt
    ¼ teaspoon cloves
   1½ cups dairy sour cream
      1 cup raisins

OVEN 375°   9-INCH PIE

In large mixer bowl, combine eggs, sugar, cinnamon, salt and cloves; blend thoroughly at low speed. Stir in sour cream and raisins. Pour into unbaked pastry shell. Bake at 375° for 35 to 45 minutes until knife inserted near center comes out clean. Cool. Serve with whipped cream, if desired.

Chocolate chips and crisp pecans melt together deliciously. You can richly finish it off with whipped cream.

Pecan Chip Pie

9-inch Unbaked Pastry Shell, see page 63

      3 eggs
      1 cup light corn syrup
    ½ cup sugar
    ⅛ teaspoon salt
      1 teaspoon vanilla
      1 cup chopped pecans
    ½ cup semi-sweet chocolate pieces

OVEN 375°   9-INCH PIE

In large mixer bowl, combine eggs, corn syrup, sugar, salt and vanilla. Blend well at medium speed. Stir in pecans and chocolate pieces. Pour into unbaked pastry shell. Bake at 375° for 40 to 45 minutes until knife inserted near center comes out clean. Cool. Serve plain or with whipped cream.

A delectable combination of chocolatey fudge and golden, chewy pecan topping nestled on a light pastry crust.

Black Bottom Pecan Pie

8-inch Unbaked Pastry Shell, see page 63

Fudge Filling
    ¾ cup sugar
    ¼ cup cocoa
    ¼ teaspoon salt
      3 tablespoons butter or margarine,
         softened
    ½ teaspoon vanilla
      2 eggs

Pecan Topping
    ¼ cup sugar
    ½ cup light corn syrup
      1 tablespoon butter or margarine,
         softened
      1 teaspoon vanilla
      2 eggs
      1 cup pecan halves

OVEN 350°   8-INCH PIE

Fudge Filling: In small mixer bowl, combine all Fudge Filling ingredients. Blend well at medium speed. Pour into unbaked pastry shell. Bake at 350° for 20 minutes. Spoon Pecan Topping over partially baked pie. Bake at 350° for 30 to 35 minutes until crust is golden brown. If desired, serve with whipped cream or ice cream.

Pecan Topping: In small mixer bowl, combine all ingredients except pecan halves. Blend well at medium speed. Stir in pecans.

A kicky combination of holiday ingredients that's sure to please. It features a seasoned pastry shell.

Pumpkin-Nog Pie

Pastry Shell and Filling
   9-inch Unbaked Pastry Shell, see below
   ½ teaspoon pumpkin pie spice
   2 eggs
   I can (I lb. 2 oz.) pumpkin pie mix
   I cup prepared egg nog

Egg Nog Topping
   I envelope whipped topping mix
   ¼ cup milk
   ¼ cup prepared egg nog
   I teaspoon vanilla

OVEN 400°   9-INCH PIE

Shell and Filling: Prepare 9-inch unbaked pastry shell as directed on page 63 adding ½ teaspoon pumpkin pie spice to flour mixture. In mixing bowl, combine eggs, pumpkin pie filling and egg nog. Beat until thoroughly blended. Pour into unbaked pastry shell. Bake at 400° for 45 to 50 minutes until knife comes out clean when inserted near center. Cool. Just before serving, spoon Egg Nog Topping around edge of pie.

Egg Nog Topping: In small mixer bowl, combine all ingredients. Beat at medium speed until peaks form.

Tip: This is the pumpkin pie mix with sugar and spices added, you add eggs and liquid.

84

Creamy pumpkin filling made easy with a mix on a layer of rich chewy pecans . . . for a double delight on an old holiday favorite.

Praline Pumpkin-Custard Pie

9-inch Unbaked Pastry Shell, see page 63

    ⅓ cup chopped pecans
    ⅓ cup firmly packed brown sugar
    3 tablespoons butter, softened
    I can (I lb. I4 oz.) pumpkin pie mix

OVEN 375°   9-INCH PIE

In small mixing bowl, combine pecans, brown sugar and butter. Press gently into bottom of unbaked pastry shell. Prepare pumpkin pie mix as directed on label. Pour over brown sugar mixture. Bake at 375° for 55 to 60 minutes until a knife inserted near center comes out clean. Cool.

Tip: This is the pumpkin pie mix with sugar, spices and liquid added. You just add the eggs.

Why Pilgrims loved the New World! An old-fashioned custard pie with a two-tone filling of maple and egg custard. One hour and fifteen minutes.

New England Custard Pie

9-inch Unbaked Pastry Shell, see page 63

Maple Filling

    ½ cup maple syrup
    ¼ cup water
    2 tablespoons flour
    ¼ teaspoon maple flavoring
    I egg
    I tablespoon butter or margarine

Custard Filling

    2 eggs
    ¼ cup sugar
    ¼ teaspoon salt
    I cup milk, scalded
    I cup light cream, scalded

OVEN 400°   9-INCH PIE

Maple Filling: In medium saucepan, combine maple syrup, water, flour and maple flavoring. Mix until smooth. Add egg and butter. Cook over medium heat, stirring constantly, until thickened. Pour into unbaked pastry shell. Pour Custard Filling carefully over Maple Filling. Bake at 400° for 30 to 35 minutes until a knife inserted halfway between center and edge of custard comes out clean.

Custard Filling: In small mixer bowl, combine eggs, sugar and salt. Blend well. Gradually stir in hot milk and cream.

A crazy combination of mellow pumpkin and chewy coconut . . . a great new holiday tradition you start!

Pum-Conut Pie

9-inch Unbaked Pastry Shell, see page 63

    2 eggs, slightly beaten
    I can (I lb. I4 oz.) pumpkin pie mix
    ¼ teaspoon mace
    ¾ cup flaked coconut

OVEN 375°   9-INCH PIE

In mixing bowl, combine eggs, pie mix, mace and ½ cup of the flaked coconut; blend well. Pour into unbaked pastry shell. Bake at 375° for 50 minutes; sprinkle with remaining ¼ cup coconut. Bake I0 more minutes until knife inserted near center comes out clean. Cool. Serve plain or with whipped cream.

Tips: This is the pumpkin pie mix with pumpkin, sugar, spices and liquid; you add eggs. For a spicier pie, add ½ teaspoon cinnamon and ¼ teaspoon nutmeg to pie mix.

Under the hearty pecan filling is a refreshing cream cheese filling. An extra special touch to an extra special pie.

Mystery Pecan Pie

9-inch Unbaked Pastry Shell, see page 63

    I package (8 oz.) cream cheese, softened
    ⅓ cup sugar
    ¼ teaspoon salt
    I teaspoon vanilla
    I egg
    I¼ cups pecans, chopped

Topping

    3 eggs
    ¼ cup sugar
    I cup light corn syrup
    I teaspoon vanilla

OVEN 375°   9-INCH PIE

In small mixer bowl, combine cream cheese, sugar, salt, vanilla and egg. Blend well at medium speed. Spread in bottom of unbaked pastry shell. Sprinkle with pecans. Gently pour Topping over pecans. Bake at 375° for 35 to 40 minutes until center is firm to the touch.

Topping: In small mixer bowl, combine all ingredients. Blend well at medium speed.

The accent is Dixie for sure with that Southern candy brown sugar flavor. It's quick and easy to fix, too!

Southern Sugar Pie

9-inch Unbaked Pastry Shell, see page 63

    I cup sugar
    I cup firmly packed brown sugar
    ¼ cup Pillsbury's Best All Purpose Flour*
    ½ teaspoon salt
    4 eggs
    ½ cup butter or margarine, melted
    ½ cup milk
    I tablespoon vanilla

OVEN 350°   9-INCH PIE

In large mixer bowl, combine sugar, brown sugar, flour, salt and eggs; blend well at medium speed. Stir in butter, milk and vanilla. Pour into unbaked pastry shell. Bake at 350° for 45 to 55 minutes until knife inserted near center comes out clean.

*For use with Pillsbury's Best Self-Rising Flour, omit salt.

Mystery Pecan Pie

A layer of chocolate tucked between velvet custard and a blanket of meringue. Surprise? A delight!

Chocolate Surprise Custard Pie

8-inch Unbaked Pastry Shell, see page 63

       1 egg
       3 egg yolks
    ½ cup sugar
       1 teaspoon vanilla
    1¾ cup milk, scalded
       2 squares (1 oz. each) semi-sweet
          chocolate, shaved or grated

3-egg white Meringue, see page 65

OVEN 400°   8-INCH PIE

In small mixing bowl, combine egg, egg yolks, sugar and vanilla; beat with fork until well blended. Gradually add hot milk; stir well. Add chocolate. Do not stir. Carefully pour into unbaked pastry shell. Bake at 400° for 30 to 35 minutes until knife inserted near center comes out clean. Cover with Meringue. Bake at 375° for 8 to 10 minutes until lightly browned.

Tip: The pastry with vinegar added, see page 63, makes a nice crust for this pie.

Chewy peanuts and crisp, coconut flakes highlight this simple and delicious pie. Tastes a lot like pecan pie but it's peanut!

Pea-Co-Nut Pie

9-inch Unbaked Pastry Shell, see page 63

       3 eggs
       1 cup light corn syrup
    ¼ cup sugar
    ⅛ teaspoon salt
       2 tablespoons butter, softened
       1 teaspoon vanilla
       1 cup cocktail peanuts
    ½ cup flaked coconut

OVEN 375°   9-INCH PIE

In large mixer bowl, combine eggs, corn syrup, sugar, salt, butter and vanilla. Blend well at medium speed. Stir in peanuts and coconut. Pour into unbaked pastry shell. Bake at 375° for 35 to 45 minutes until crust is golden brown. Cool thoroughly for several hours. If desired, serve with whipped cream.

Pea-Co-Nut Pie

Meringue Pies

Sugar and spice and pumpkin cream so nice tucked away between a light, pastry shell and high, light meringue.

Snow Capped Pumpkin Pie

9-inch Baked Pastry Shell, see page 63

    1½ cups canned or cooked pumpkin
    3 egg yolks
    ¾ cup sugar
    ⅔ cup (6 oz. can) evaporated milk
    2 tablespoons butter or margarine
    1 teaspoon cinnamon
    ½ teaspoon nutmeg
    ¼ teaspoon salt
    ¼ teaspoon ginger
    3 egg white Meringue, see page 65

OVEN 350°   9-INCH PIE

In medium saucepan, combine pumpkin, egg yolks, sugar, milk, butter, cinnamon, nutmeg, salt and ginger. Bring to a boil. Cook, stirring constantly, until thick. Cool slightly; pour into baked pastry shell. Top with Meringue, sealing edges well. Sprinkle with additional nutmeg. Bake at 350° for 12 to 15 minutes until golden brown.

Ho ho ho and a rum-flavored coconut cream pie, that is topped off with a high meringue.

Pirates Prize Coconut Pie

9-inch Baked Pastry Shell, see page 63

Coconut Cream Filling

    1 cup sugar
    ½ cup Pillsbury's Best All Purpose Flour*
    ¼ teaspoon salt
    1 cup flaked or shredded coconut
    3 cups milk
    3 egg yolks, slightly beaten
    ½ teaspoon rum flavoring
    3 egg white Meringue, see page 65

9-INCH PIE

Coconut Cream Filling: In saucepan, combine sugar, flour, salt and coconut. Add milk gradually, mixing well. Cook over medium heat, stirring constantly, until mixture boils and is thick. Add a little of the hot mixture to egg yolks; add to remaining hot mixture. Cook for 2 minutes over medium heat, stirring constantly. Add rum flavoring. Cover and cool. Pour into baked pastry shell. Spread on Meringue, sealing to edge of crust. Bake at 350° for 10 to 12 minutes, until lightly browned.

Tip: If desired, substitute 2 tablespoons dark rum for rum flavoring in filling.

*For use with Pillsbury's Best Self-Rising Flour, omit salt.

For a luau or luncheon, this tangy blend of lemon and pineapple makes lemon meringue pie special.

Tangy Hawaiian Pie

9-inch Baked Pastry Shell, see page 63

    1 package (3½ oz.) lemon pudding and
      pie filling mix
  ½ cup sugar
1¾ cups water
    1 can (8½ oz.) or 1 cup crushed pineapple,
      undrained
    2 egg yolks
    2 teaspoons grated lemon peel, if desired

Meringue
    2 egg whites
  ⅛ teaspoon cream of tartar
  ¼ cup sugar

OVEN 350°   9-INCH PIE

In saucepan, combine pie filling mix and sugar; stir in ¼ cup water. Add remaining water, crushed pineapple, egg yolks and lemon peel; mix well. Cook over medium heat, stirring occasionally, until thick. Cool to lukewarm. Turn into baked pastry shell; cover with Meringue, sealing to edges. Bake at 350° for 10 to 12 minutes until lightly browned. Cool.

Meringue: In small mixer bowl, beat egg whites and cream of tartar at high speed until soft peaks form; add sugar gradually, beating until stiff.

Looks and tastes like pineapple meringue, but it's easy . . . pineapple and sour cream filling, no-fail meringue.

Magic Meringue Pie

9-inch Baked Pastry Shell, see page 63

Pineapple Filling
　¾ cup sugar
　2 tablespoons flour
　⅛ teaspoon salt
　I can (I lb. 4 oz.) crushed pineapple,
　　drain, reserve ½ cup syrup
　I cup dairy sour cream
　3 egg yolks
　I tablespoon lemon juice

Never Fail Meringue
　2 tablespoons sugar
　I tablespoon cornstarch
　½ cup water
　3 egg whites
　⅛ teaspoon salt
　½ teaspoon vanilla
　⅓ cup sugar

OVEN 350°　　　　　　　　9-INCH PIE

Pineapple Filling: In saucepan, combine sugar, flour and salt. Add crushed pineapple, reserved ½ cup syrup, sour cream, egg yolks and lemon juice. Cook over medium heat, stirring constantly, until mixture boils and is thick. Cover and cool. Pour into baked pastry shell. Top with Never Fail Meringue. Bake at 350° for 12 to 15 minutes, until golden brown.

Never Fail Meringue: In small saucepan, combine sugar and cornstarch. Add water; cook over medium heat, stirring constantly until mixture is thick and clear. Cool. In small mixer bowl, combine egg whites, salt and vanilla. Beat at high speed until foamy. Add sugar gradually, beating after each addition. Add cornstarch mixture. Continue beating until meringue stands in stiff peaks.

Tip: If desired, top with a 3 egg white Meringue. (see page 65)

The flavors are delicious together: tart lemon filling over a spicy mincemeat surprise topped with light and lovely meringue.

Lemon Surprise Pie

9-inch Baked Pastry Shell, see page 63

　I cup prepared mincemeat
　I cup sugar
　¼ cup cornstarch
　I½ cups water
　I tablespoon grated lemon peel
　⅓ cup lemon juice
　3 egg yolks, slightly beaten
　I tablespoon butter or margarine

3 egg white Meringue, see page 65

OVEN 350°　　　　　　　　9-INCH PIE

Spread mincemeat over bottom of baked pastry shell. In saucepan, combine sugar and cornstarch. Stir in water, grated lemon peel and juice. Cook over medium heat, stirring constantly, until thick. Blend a little of the hot mixture into beaten egg yolks. Add to remaining hot mixture; cook, stirring constantly, 2 minutes. Stir in butter. Cool. Pour over mincemeat. Top with Meringue. Bake at 350° for 12 to 15 minutes, until Meringue is lightly browned. Cool before serving.

Tip: I package (3½ oz.) lemon pudding and pie filling mix may be used. Prepare as directed on package for pie filling. Pour over mincemeat in pastry shell.

Creamy custard filling rests on a bed of chewy coconut. Then you top it off with high and handsome meringue.

Custard Snow Pie

9-inch Baked Pastry Shell, see page 63

Custard Snow Filling
   3 egg yolks
 1½ cups milk
  ¾ cup sugar
  ¼ cup Pillsbury's Best All Purpose Flour*
  ½ teaspoon salt
   1 teaspoon vanilla
   1 cup flaked coconut
   3 egg white Meringue, see page 65

OVEN 350°   9-INCH PIE

Custard Snow Filling: In medium saucepan, combine egg yolks, milk, sugar, flour and salt. Bring to a rolling boil, stirring constantly. Continue cooking until thick. Remove from heat. Stir in vanilla. Cool slightly. Sprinkle coconut in bottom of baked pastry shell. Pour in filling. Top with Meringue. Bake at 350° for 10 to 12 minutes until lightly browned.

Tip: 1 package (3¼ oz.) vanilla or coconut pudding and pie filling mix may be used for Custard Snow Filling. Prepare as directed on package.

*For use with Pillsbury's Best Self-Rising Flour, omit salt in the Custard Snow Filling.

Under the easy-mix meringue is a smooth orange filling captured in a distinctive orange crust. Ready to chill in a little over an hour.

Sub-Meringue Pie

Pastry Shell
   1 package Pillsbury Pie Crust Mix or Sticks
   1 teaspoon grated orange peel
   2 teaspoons butter, melted
   2 tablespoons orange juice

Filling
   1 package (3 oz.) vanilla pudding and pie
     filling mix
 1¼ cups milk
  ¾ cup orange juice
   1 tablespoon grated orange peel
   1 package Pillsbury Fluffy White
     Frosting Mix

OVEN 450°   9-INCH PIE

Pastry Shell: In small mixing bowl, combine ⅔ cup firmly packed pie crust mix or one pie crust stick and orange peel. Mix butter and orange juice; add to mix and stir with a fork until dough holds together. Form into a ball. Roll out on floured surface to a circle 1 inch larger than inverted 9-inch pie pan. Fold pastry in half and transfer to pie pan, unfold and fit loosely into pan, gently patting out any air pockets. Fold edges to form a standing rim; flute. Prick bottom and sides generously with fork. Bake at 450° for 8 to 10 minutes, until golden brown. Cool.

Filling: In saucepan, combine pudding mix, milk, orange juice and orange peel. Cook over medium heat, stirring constantly until thick and smooth. Cool. Prepare frosting mix as directed on package. Fold ½ cup gently but thoroughly into orange pudding. Pour into cooled pastry shell. Top with remaining fluffy frosting. Bake at 350° for 12 to 15 minutes or until lightly browned. Chill 3 to 4 hours before serving.

Zesty cinnamon-flavored meringue piled high on rosy-hued rhubarb cream. Inviting . . . delicious.

Cinna-Meringue Rhubarb Pie

9-inch Baked Pastry Shell, see page 63

    ½ cup sugar
 2½ tablespoons cornstarch
    ¼ cup light cream
     I package (I lb.) frozen rhubarb, thawed
     I tablespoon butter or margarine
     3 egg yolks, slightly beaten
     I teaspoon vanilla
     6 to 8 drops red food coloring, if desired

Meringue

     3 egg whites
    ¼ teaspoon cream of tartar
    ¼ teaspoon cinnamon
    ⅓ cup sugar

OVEN 350°   9-INCH PIE

In saucepan, combine sugar and cornstarch. Add cream, rhubarb and butter; mix well. Cook over medium heat, stirring occasionally, until mixture comes to a boil. Blend a small amount of hot mixture into egg yolks; add to hot mixture. Cook over medium heat 2 minutes, stirring constantly. Add vanilla and food coloring; cool to lukewarm. Pour into baked pastry shell; top with Meringue, sealing to edge. Bake at 350° for 10 to 12 minutes until lightly browned. Cool.

Meringue: In small mixer bowl, beat egg whites with cream of tartar and cinnamon at high speed until soft peaks form. Add sugar gradually; beat until stiff.

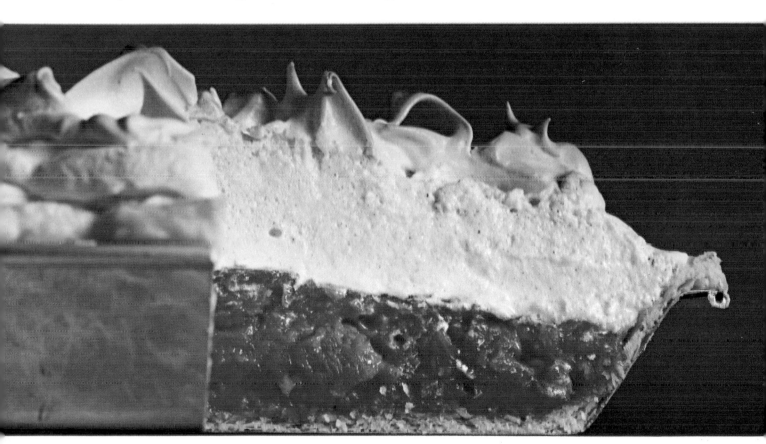

Chilled Pies

Soda fountain delight! A mellow filling of chocolate, marshmallows and malt—piled high in a one-crust pie; pecans add the finishing touch.

Chocolate Mallow Malt Pie

9-inch Baked Pastry Shell, see page 63

   2 cups miniature marshmallows
  ½ cup semi-sweet chocolate pieces
  ½ cup milk
  ¼ teaspoon salt
   I cup whipping cream
  ¼ cup chocolate or vanilla malted milk
    powder
   I teaspoon vanilla
  ¼ cup chopped pecans

9-INCH PIE

In top of double boiler, combine marshmallows, chocolate pieces, milk and salt. Cook over hot water, stirring occasionally, until marshmallows and chocolate are melted. Remove from heat; cool until slightly thickened. In small mixer bowl, combine whipping cream, malted milk powder and vanilla. Beat until very thick. Fold in chocolate-marshmallow mixture. Spoon into baked pastry shell. Sprinkle chopped pecans around edge of pie. Chill at least 3 hours before serving.

A layer of thickened glazed blueberries tucked between blankets of whipped cream. Refreshing and light—blueberries and cream.

Freshy's Blueberry Pie

9-inch Baked Pastry Shell, see page 63

    ¾ cup sugar
    3 tablespoons cornstarch
    ¼ teaspoon salt
    ½ cup water
    I package (I2 oz.) frozen blueberries
    I tablespoon lemon juice
    2 tablespoons butter or margarine
    I cup whipping cream
    2 tablespoons confectioners' sugar
    ½ teaspoon vanilla

                                    9-INCH PIE

In saucepan, combine sugar, cornstarch and salt. Add water, blueberries and lemon juice. Cook over medium heat, stirring occasionally, until mixture is thick. Add butter. Cool. In small mixer bowl, combine whipping cream, confectioners' sugar and vanilla. Beat until thickened. Spread half of whipped cream mixture in bottom of baked pastry shell. Top with blueberry mixture. Chill I to 2 hours before serving. Top with remaining whipped cream.

A new twist to a cheese pie — orange cream cheese filling plays middleman to a chocolate crust and a whipped cream topping.

Orange Cheese Pie

9-inch Baked Chocolate Pastry Shell, see page 63

    I package (8 oz.) cream cheese, softened
    2 tablespoons milk
    2 eggs
    ⅓ cup sugar
    I tablespoon grated orange peel
    I teaspoon vanilla
    ½ cup cut-up orange sections
    ¼ cup chopped toasted almonds

Topping

    I cup whipping cream
    2 tablespoons sugar
    2 tablespoons grated orange peel

OVEN 350°   9-INCH PIE

In small mixer bowl, beat cream cheese with milk at medium speed until fluffy. Add eggs; beat well at high speed. Blend in sugar, orange peel and vanilla; fold in orange sections. Pour into baked chocolate crust; bake at 350° for I5 to 20 minutes until firm. Cool. Chill several hours or overnight. Spread with Topping; sprinkle with chopped almonds.

Topping: In small mixing bowl, beat all ingredients until thick.

Tips: ½ cup mandarin orange sections may be substituted for cut-up orange sections.

If desired, use a 9-inch baked pastry shell for chocolate pastry.

Pineapple cheese lines a pie and holds a center of juicy blueberry filling . . . all in a crust, for pretty pie-shaped servings.

Cream Around A Berry Pie

9-inch Baked Pastry Shell, see page 63

Pineapple Filling

    I package (8 oz.) cream cheese, softened
    3 tablespoons sugar
    I tablespoon milk
    ½ teaspoon vanilla
    I can (8½ oz.) crushed pineapple, drain
      and reserve syrup

Blueberry Filling

    2 tablespoons cornstarch
    2 tablespoons sugar
    ¼ teaspoon salt
    I can (I5 oz.) blueberries, drain and
      reserve syrup
    I tablespoon butter
    I teaspoon lemon juice

                                    9-INCH PIE

Pineapple Filling: In small mixer bowl, blend cream cheese, sugar, milk and vanilla. Stir in drained pineapple. Spread over bottom and sides of baked pastry shell. Pour Blueberry Filling in center. Chill at least 4 hours.

Blueberry Filling: In medium saucepan, combine cornstarch, sugar and salt. Combine pineapple syrup and blueberry syrup, adding water to make I½ cups. Stir into cornstarch mixture. Cook over medium heat, stirring constantly, until thick and clear. Stir in butter, lemon juice and blueberries. Cool.

A dark chocolate cookie crust holds a light and lively custard chiffon. Easy-made with packaged mixes in 20 minutes. Chills only an hour, or longer if you wish.

Chocolate Crusted Pie

9-inch Chocolate Cookie Crust, see page 65
  1¾ cups milk
    1 package (3¾ oz.) vanilla instant
      pudding mix
    1 package (2 oz.) whipped topping mix

9-INCH PIE

In small mixer bowl, combine milk, pudding mix and topping mix at lowest speed until all ingredients are moistened. Beat at high speed until soft mounds form. Spoon into Chocolate Cookie Crust. Garnish with a few additional cookie crumbs. Chill at least 1 hour before serving.

Tip: Try this pie filling idea with other flavors of instant pudding.

A quick and easy way to caramel cream pie . . . pudding mix and ice cream topping. Bananas and special topping make it extra special.

Banana Caramel Cream Pie

<u>9-inch Baked Pastry Shell</u>, see page 63

<u>Filling</u>
    1 package (3¼ oz.) vanilla pudding and
      pie filling mix
    2 cups milk
    ¼ cup caramel ice cream topping
    2 bananas, sliced

<u>Caramel Cream Topping</u>
    ½ cup whipping cream
    2 tablespoons firmly packed brown sugar

9-INCH PIE

<u>Filling</u>: In saucepan, combine pudding mix, milk and caramel topping. Cook over medium heat, stirring occasionally, until thick and bubbly. Cool. Arrange banana slices in baked pastry shell; cover with pudding. Garnish with Topping and additional banana slices, if desired.

<u>Caramel Cream Topping</u>: In small mixing bowl, combine whipping cream and brown sugar; beat until thick.

A really good-tasting prune dessert, made ever-so-easy with prepared prune filling and whipped dessert mix. Less than an hour until it's ready to chill.

Prune Whip Pie

<u>9-inch Baked Pastry Shell</u>, see page 63
    1 can (12 oz.) prune cake and pastry filling
    1 package (3¾ oz.) vanilla whipped
      dessert mix
    1 can (12 oz.) almond cake and pastry
      filling
    Slivered almonds or grated sweet
      chocolate

9-INCH PIE

Spread prune filling over bottom and sides of baked pastry shell. Prepare dessert mix as directed on package. Beat in almond cake and pastry filling. Pour over prune filling. Chill at least 2 hours before serving. Garnish with slivered almonds or grated sweet chocolate.

Sliced peaches separate a layer of lime cream cheese and lime chiffon. Chilly and beautiful, garnished with more peach slices.

Peachy Lime Mist Pie

<u>9-inch Baked Pastry Shell</u>, see page 63
    ½ cup sugar
    1 envelope (1 tablespoon) unflavored
      gelatin
    1 teaspoon grated lime peel
    ¼ teaspoon salt
    4 egg yolks, slightly beaten
    ½ cup water or syrup from peaches
    ⅓ cup lime juice
    1 package (8 oz.) cream cheese, softened
    ¼ cup sugar
    1 can (1 lb. 13 oz.) peach slices, drained
    4 egg whites
    ½ cup sugar

9-INCH PIE

In top of double boiler, combine ½ cup sugar, gelatin, lime peel and salt. Stir in egg yolks, water and lime juice. Cook over boiling water, stirring occasionally, until mixture is slightly thickened. Remove from heat.

In small mixer bowl, combine cream cheese and ¼ cup sugar. Add ⅓ cup of gelatin mixture; mix until smooth. Spread in bottom of baked pastry shell. Chill until firm. Chill remaining gelatin mixture until thick, but not set.

Arrange drained peach slices over cream cheese mixture, reserving 6 slices for garnish. In small mixer bowl, beat egg whites until foamy. Add ½ cup sugar gradually, beating until stiff, glossy peaks form. Fold in gelatin mixture. Spoon over peaches. Garnish with peach slices. Chill at least 2 hours before serving.

A lime pie—pretty as a picture yet unbelievably simple. A cool refresher after a hearty meal.

Limelight Pie

8-inch Baked Pastry Shell, see page 63
> 1 can (15 oz.) or 1⅓ cups sweetened condensed milk
> ⅓ cup lime juice
> ¼ teaspoon salt
> 1 can (8 oz.) crushed pineapple, drained (⅔ cup)
> 2 to 4 drops green food coloring
> Whipped cream

8-INCH PIE

In small mixing bowl, combine condensed milk, lime juice and salt; stir until thickened. Blend in pineapple and food coloring. Spread in baked pastry shell. Chill 2 to 3 hours. Serve with whipped cream. If desired, garnish with grated chocolate or chocolate curls.

Tip: An 8-inch Baked Chocolate Pastry Shell, see page 63, may be substituted for 8-inch Baked Pastry Shell.

Pumpkin and butterscotch team up with cream cheese to make this a pleasant new flavor experience, fit for Prince Charming.

Cinderella Cheesepie

9-inch Baked Pastry Shell, see page 63
> 1 package (4 oz.) butterscotch pudding and pie filling mix
> 1 can (1 lb. 2 oz.) pumpkin pie mix
> 2 egg yolks
> 1 envelope (1 tablespoon) unflavored gelatin
> 1½ cups milk
> 1 package (3 oz.) cream cheese
> 2 egg whites

9-INCH PIE

In saucepan, combine pudding mix, pumpkin pie mix, egg yolks, unflavored gelatin and milk. Mix until well blended and smooth. Cook over medium heat, stirring constantly, until mixture thickens and comes to a boil. Remove from heat. Add cream cheese; allow to soften, then beat with rotary beater until smooth. Chill until slightly thickened but not set. In small

mixer bowl, beat egg whites until stiff but not dry; fold into pumpkin mixture. Spoon filling into baked pastry shell. Chill at least 3 hours or overnight before serving. Serve with whipped cream, if desired.

Tips: This is the pumpkin pie mix with pumpkin, sugar and spices; you add the eggs and liquid.

1 can (1 lb.) pumpkin may be used. Add ½ cup sugar, 1 teaspoon cinnamon, ¼ teaspoon nutmeg and ¼ teaspoon ginger.

A chiffon pie made with butterscotch morsels, sprinkled with walnuts. Allow an hour to make; 2 hours to chill.

Butterscotch Walnut Pie

9-inch Baked Graham Cracker Crust, see page 65
> 1 envelope (1 tablespoon) unflavored gelatin
> ¼ cup cold water
> 1 package (6 oz.) or 1 cup butterscotch morsels
> 1 package (3 oz.) cream cheese, softened
> ½ cup chopped walnuts
> ½ cup milk
> 3 egg yolks
> ½ teaspoon rum flavoring
> 3 egg whites
> ¼ cup sugar
> 2 tablespoons chopped walnuts

9-INCH PIE

In medium saucepan, soften gelatin in cold water; place over medium heat to dissolve gelatin. Stir in morsels and cream cheese; mix well. Remove from heat. Add walnuts, milk, egg yolks and rum flavoring; mix well. Chill until very thick but not set. In small mixer bowl, beat egg whites at high speed until soft mounds form. Add sugar gradually; beat until stiff. Fold into butterscotch mixture. Spoon into graham cracker crust. Sprinkle with walnuts. Chill at least 2 hours.

Skillet-browned crumb crust filled with sour cream instant pudding, crowned with mandarin oranges and marmalade glaze. Make it in 30 to 45 minutes and chill.

Mandarin Dream Pie

Crust
- ⅓ cup butter
- ¾ cup Pillsbury's Best All Purpose or Self-Rising Flour
- ¼ cup firmly packed brown sugar
- ⅛ teaspoon ginger
- ½ cup finely chopped nuts

Filling
- I cup dairy sour cream
- ¾ cup milk
- I tablespoon grated orange peel
- I package (3¾ oz.) instant vanilla pudding
- I can (II oz.) mandarin oranges, drain and reserve I tablespoon syrup
- ½ cup orange marmalade

<u>Crust</u>: In heavy skillet, melt butter. Stir in flour, brown sugar, ginger and chopped nuts; blend well. Cook over low heat, stirring constantly, until crumbs are toasted and golden brown. Cool. Press crumb mixture onto bottom and up sides of 8-inch pie pan.

<u>Filling</u>: In small mixer bowl, combine sour cream, milk, orange peel and pudding mix. Mix at low speed to blend. Beat at high speed, about 30 seconds or until thickened. *Do not overmix.* Pour into crumb crust. Chill until set.

Arrange mandarin oranges on top of filling. In small saucepan, combine orange marmalade and I tablespoon of reserved syrup. Cook over low heat, stirring constantly until marmalade melts; spoon over oranges to cover. Chill until served.

<u>Tip</u>: *If desired, use an 8-inch baked pastry shell for crust above.*

Fresh strawberries and currant jelly team up for a sensational glaze on a sour cream-gelatin filling. Cuts well into pretty servings.

Strawberry Devonshire Pie

9-inch Baked Pastry Shell, see page 63

- 1 envelope (1 tablespoon) unflavored gelatin
- ¼ cup cold water
- 1 cup dairy sour cream
- 2 egg yolks
- 2 tablespoons sugar
- 2 tablespoons milk
- ⅛ teaspoon salt
- 2 egg whites
- ¼ teaspoon almond extract
- ¼ cup sugar
- 1 cup fresh strawberry halves
- ½ cup red currant jelly
- 1 tablespoon water

Soften gelatin in water. In saucepan, combine sour cream, egg yolks, sugar, milk and salt; mix well. Cook over medium heat, stirring constantly, 5 minutes. Blend in gelatin. Cool, stirring occasionally, until thick but not set. In small mixer bowl, beat egg whites with almond extract at high speed until soft mounds form. Gradually add ¼ cup sugar, beating until stiff, glossy peaks form. Fold into chilled mixture gently but thoroughly. Spoon into baked pastry shell. Chill until set, about 2 hours. Arrange strawberry halves on top of pie. Heat jelly with water, stirring constantly until jelly melts; spoon over strawberries. Chill until served.

Cookie crust with coconut supports a high, golden pineapple cream filling, topped with crumbs and ringed with crushed pineapple. Allow at least 2 hours for chilling.

Pineapple Paradise Pie

Crust
> 1 cup Pillsbury's Best All Purpose or
>   Self-Rising Flour
> ½ cup flaked coconut
> ¼ cup firmly packed brown sugar
> ½ cup butter or margarine, softened

Pineapple Cream Filling
> ½ cup firmly packed brown sugar
> 3 tablespoons flour*
> ¼ teaspoon salt
> 1 can (1 lb. 4 oz.) crushed pineapple,
>   drain and reserve ¾ cup of syrup
> ¾ cup milk
> 2 eggs, slightly beaten
> 2 tablespoons butter or margarine
> ½ cup whipping cream

OVEN 400°   9-INCH PIE

Crust: In small mixer bowl, combine crust ingredients. Mix at low speed until ingredients are well blended. Press into bottom of 13x9-inch pan. Bake at 400° for 12 to 14 minutes, until golden brown. Cool. With fork, crumble mixture. Press 2 cups of crumb mixture into 9-inch pie pan; reserve remaining mixture for topping.

Pineapple Cream Filling: In saucepan, combine brown sugar, flour and salt. Gradually stir in pineapple syrup and milk. Cook over medium heat, stirring constantly, until thick. Blend small amount of hot mixture into eggs; add to mixture in saucepan. Cook 2 minutes over medium heat, stirring constantly. Stir in butter. Reserve ½ cup of pineapple; blend remainder into filling. Cool completely. Pour into crumb crust. In small mixer bowl, beat cream until thick. Spread over filling; sprinkle with reserved crumb mixture. Arrange reserved ½ cup crushed pineapple around edge of pie. Chill at least 2 hours before serving.

Tip: If desired, use Pineapple Cream Filling in baked 9-inch pastry shell. Omit crumb topping.

*For use with Pillsbury's Best Self-Rising Flour, omit salt in Pineapple Cream Filling.

Can you imagine fluffy frosting folded into pineapple-lemon gelatin? It tastes deliciously rich . . . looks gorgeous.

Imagination Pie

9-inch Baked Pastry Shell, see page 63
> 1 can (8½ oz.) crushed pineapple, drain
>   and reserve syrup
> ¼ cup water
> 1 package (3 oz.) lemon-flavored gelatin
> 1 cup evaporated milk or light cream
> 1 package Pillsbury Fluffy White Frosting
>   Mix

9-INCH PIE

In saucepan, combine reserved pineapple syrup and water. Bring to a boil. In large mixing bowl, dissolve gelatin in hot liquids. Add evaporated milk. Chill, stirring occasionally, until partially set. Prepare frosting mix as directed on package. Fold pineapple and frosting into gelatin mixture. Pour into baked pastry shell. Chill at least 2 hours before serving. Serve with whipped cream, if desired.

Chocolate and coffee combine to make a smooth filling for this chilled cream pie. Marshmallows make it easy.

Mocha Frappé Pie

9-inch Baked Pastry Shell, see page 63
> ½ lb. (about 40) large marshmallows
> ¼ cup sugar
> ½ cup evaporated milk
> 2 teaspoons instant coffee
> 1 cup (6 oz. package) semi-sweet
>   chocolate pieces
> 1 cup whipping cream

9-INCH PIE

In top of double boiler, combine marshmallows, sugar, evaporated milk and instant coffee. Cook over boiling water, stirring occasionally, until marshmallows are melted. Remove from heat. Stir in semi-sweet chocolate pieces. Cool. Spread ¾ cup of filling in bottom of baked pastry shell. Beat whipping cream until thick. Fold in remaining chocolate mixture. Pour over chocolate layer. Chill at least 2 hours before serving. If desired, serve with whipped cream.

This special lemon pie has cream cheese and meringue in the filling. A cool smoothie for your next bridge luncheon—the family will love it, too.

Lemon Cloud Pie

9-inch Baked Pastry Shell, see page 63

  ¾ cup sugar
  3 tablespoons cornstarch
  I cup water
  I teaspoon grated lemon peel
  ¼ to ⅓ cup lemon juice
  2 egg yolks, slightly beaten
  I package (3 oz.) cream cheese
  2 egg whites
  ¼ cup sugar

9-INCH PIE

In saucepan, combine ¾ cup sugar, cornstarch, water, lemon peel, lemon juice and slightly beaten egg yolks. Beat with rotary beater until well blended. Cook over medium heat, stirring constantly, until thick. Remove from heat. Add cream cheese; stir until well blended. Cool while preparing meringue. In small mixer bowl, beat egg whites at high speed, until foamy. Add ¼ cup sugar gradually, continuing to beat until meringue stands in stiff, glossy peaks. Fold into lemon mixture. Spoon into baked pastry shell. Chill at least 2 hours before serving.

Sunshine bright colors with a summer-cool refreshing taste. Sour cream makes it special.

Lemon Luscious Pie

9-inch Baked Pastry Shell, see page 63

  I cup sugar
  3 tablespoons cornstarch
  I tablespoon grated lemon peel
  ¼ cup butter
  ¼ cup lemon juice
  I cup milk
  3 egg yolks, slightly beaten
  I cup dairy sour cream

9-INCH PIE

In saucepan, combine sugar, cornstarch, lemon peel, butter, lemon juice, milk and egg yolks. Cook over medium heat, stirring constantly until thick. Cover and cool. Fold in sour cream; pour into baked pastry shell. Chill at least 2 hours before serving. Top with whipped cream.

Lemon Luscious Pie

Fruit salad a la dessert! A cool refresher studded with fruit and topped with tangy crumbs of cheese crackers.

Fruit In Cream Pie

<u>8-inch Baked Pastry Shell</u>, *see page 63*

  1½ *cups sliced bananas*
    1 cup sliced peaches, well drained
  ½ *cup miniature marshmallows*
  ½ *cup maraschino cherries, halved and*
    drained
  3 *tablespoons lemon juice*
  3 *tablespoons honey*
  ½ *cup whipping cream*
  2 *tablespoons crushed cheese crackers*

8-INCH PIE

In mixing bowl, combine bananas, peaches, marshmallows, maraschino cherries, lemon juice and honey. Chill until serving time, drain. Beat whipping cream until thick; fold into the fruit mixture. Spoon into baked pastry shell; sprinkle with cheese crackers.

<u>Tip:</u> *1 envelope whipped topping mix may be substituted for whipping cream. Prepare as directed on package.*

A pink and gold masterpiece of plump sweet peaches tucked into lush coconut cream, covered with pink peach glaze.

Peaches 'N Creamy Coconut Pie

<u>9-inch Baked Pastry Shell</u>, see page 63
    1 package (3¼ oz.) coconut pudding and
      pie filling mix
    2 cups milk
    1 can (1 lb.) peach slices,
      drain and reserve ¾ cup syrup

<u>Pink Peach Glaze</u>
    1 tablespoon cornstarch
    ¾ cup reserved syrup
    ½ teaspoon grated lemon peel
    3 drops red food coloring
    2 drops almond extract

9-INCH PIE

In saucepan, combine pudding and pie filling mix and milk. Cook as directed on package. Cool. Pour into baked pastry shell. Arrange drained peach slices on filling; top with Pink Peach Glaze. Chill several hours before serving.

Pink Peach Glaze: In small saucepan, combine cornstarch and reserved syrup. Cook over low heat until thick. Add lemon peel, red food coloring and almond extract; mix well.

Tip: Vanilla pudding and pie filling may be used. Add 1 cup flaked coconut after cooking.

Light and tasty because the chocolate is tempered with the tang of sour cream and sweet honey. Top it off with mounds of whipped cream and toasted almonds.

Honey Chocolette Pie

<u>8 or 9-inch pastry shell</u>, see below
    ¼ cup slivered almonds

<u>Chocolate Filling</u>
    1 package (6 oz.) or 1 cup semi-sweet
      chocolate pieces
    2 eggs, separated
    ½ cup dairy sour cream
    ¼ teaspoon salt
    ⅓ cup honey

8 OR 9-INCH PIE

Prepare baked pastry shell as directed on page 63, pressing almonds gently into bottom of pie shell before baking. Spoon Chocolate Filling into cooled pastry shell. Chill at least 2 hours. Garnish with whipped cream and toasted slivered almonds.

Chocolate Filling: In saucepan, melt chocolate pieces over low heat. Add egg yolks; stir until mixture leaves sides of pan in smooth compact ball. Remove from heat. Blend in sour cream; beat until smooth. In small mixer bowl, beat egg whites and salt until stiff but not dry. Add honey very slowly, beating well after each addition. Continue beating until stiff, glossy peaks form. Fold into chocolate mixture, gently but thoroughly.

The "calico" in the frothy "snow" is marshmallows, coconut and bits of chocolate. Easy chilled pie to make in an hour; allow 2 more to chill.

Calico Snow Pie

<u>9-inch Baked Pastry Shell</u>, see page 63
    1 cup whipping cream
    1 cup (7 oz. jar) marshmallow creme
    1 teaspoon vanilla
    1 cup flaked or shredded coconut
    1 square (1 oz.) semi-sweet chocolate

9-INCH PIE

In small mixer bowl, beat whipping cream until thick. Fold in marshmallow creme and vanilla. Stir in ½ cup of the coconut. Coarsely grate half of the chocolate over baked pastry shell. Sprinkle on ¼ cup of the coconut. Pour cream mixture into baked pastry shell. Grate remaining chocolate over the top; sprinkle on remaining ¼ cup coconut. Chill at least 2 hours before serving.

Make-Ahead Pies And Desserts

● As any homemaker knows, handling time is harder than handling money . . . economically. This section of desserts is for the time-wise, who want to prepare dessert ahead of time and earn themselves an extra hour when it will be most needed.

Some of these recipes can be made ahead and frozen; others are made to be mellowed in the refrigerator . . . early in the day or even the day before.

This chilled "marzipan" brownie dessert has a layer of almond filling and an almond topping. See Tip for using brownie mix or use the easy saucepan brownie. Your bridge group will love it.

Brownie Dessert Royal

Brownie
   ¾ cup butter or margarine
   3 squares (I oz. each) unsweetened
      chocolate
   I cup sugar
   3 eggs
   I cup Pillsbury's Best All Purpose Flour*
   ½ teaspoon baking powder
   I½ teaspoons vanilla

Almond Filling
   I package (3 oz.) cream cheese, softened
   I can (8 oz.) almond paste
   2 tablespoons milk

Almond Cream Topping
   I½ cups whipping cream

OVEN 350°   16 TO 18 SERVINGS

Brownie: In 2-quart saucepan, melt butter and chocolate over medium heat. Remove from heat. Blend in sugar and eggs. Add flour, baking powder and vanilla; stir until well blended. Spread half over bottom of a 13x9-inch pan which has been greased on the bottom only. Spoon Almond Filling by teaspoonfuls over Brownie mixture. Top with remaining Brownie mixture, gently spreading to cover. Bake at 350° for 25 to 30 minutes. Cool. Spread with Almond Cream Topping. Garnish with grated chocolate, if desired. Chill several hours or overnight.

Almond Filling: Combine cream cheese and half of almond paste until well blended. Gradually blend in milk.

Almond Cream Topping: Combine remaining half of almond paste and 2 tablespoons of whipping cream, just to blend. Slowly blend in remainder of cream; beat until thickened.

Tip: I package Pillsbury Family Size Brownie Mix may be substituted for brownie mixture. Prepare as directed on package, using ⅓ cup water and 2 eggs. Continue as directed above.

*For use with Pillsbury's Best Self-Rising Flour, omit baking powder in Brownie.

A rich and fluffy no-cook chocolate pie, captured in a pastry shell that hints of mint. Prepare early and chill.

Chocolate Mist Pie

9-inch Baked Pastry Shell, see below
   I teaspoon peppermint extract

Chocolate Filling
   5 egg yolks
   ¼ cup sugar
   ⅛ teaspoon salt
   I cup (6 oz. package) semi-sweet chocolate
      pieces, melted
   I teaspoon vanilla
   5 egg whites
   ¼ cup sugar

                              9-INCH PIE

Prepare baked pastry shell as directed on page 62, adding peppermint extract with water to flour mixture. Pour Chocolate Filling into cooled pastry shell. Chill for several hours until firm. Cut with a very sharp knife which has been dipped in warm water.

Chocolate Filling: In small mixer bowl, combine egg yolks, sugar and salt. Beat at high speed until thick and lemon colored. At low speed blend in melted chocolate and vanilla. In large mixer bowl, beat egg whites at high speed until soft mounds form. Gradually add sugar. Continue beating until stiff peaks form. Fold in chocolate mixture gently but thoroughly.

Tip: For a special Chocolate Mist Pie, blend in 2 to 3 tablespoons rum or brandy in place of vanilla.

Baked coconut meringue layers stacked and filled with chocolate whipped cream. Tastes especially good the next day—like layers of chocolate and marshmallow.

Chocolate Cream Torte

<u>Meringue</u>
6 egg whites
½ teaspoon salt
½ teaspoon cream of tartar
1 teaspoon almond extract
1½ cups sugar
½ cup flaked coconut

<u>Chocolate Filling</u>
1 package (6 oz.) semi-sweet chocolate pieces
1 cup miniature marshmallows
⅔ cup evaporated milk
1 cup whipping cream

OVEN 300°   10 TO 12 SERVINGS

<u>Meringue:</u> In large mixer bowl, beat egg whites, salt, cream of tartar and almond extract at high speed until soft peaks form. Gradually add sugar; continue beating until stiff peaks form. Spread Meringue on greased and floured cookie sheets, making three 6-inch circles. Bake at 300° for 25 to 30 minutes until lightly browned. Remove from cookie sheets immediately. Cool. Stack layers on serving plate, spreading Chocolate Filling between each layer and on top. Sprinkle with coconut. Chill 6 to 8 hours or overnight.

<u>Chocolate Filling:</u> In medium saucepan, heat chocolate pieces, marshmallows and milk, stirring occasionally, until melted. Chill. Beat cream until thick. Fold in chocolate mixture.

A dark, rich, silky chocolate pie sprinkled with walnuts. Serve chilly wedges on your best china, with demitasse coffee.

French Silk Chocolate Pie

<u>8-inch Baked Pastry Shell</u>, see page 63

> ¾ cup sugar
> ½ cup butter, softened
> 2 packets (1 oz. each) premelted chocolate
> 1 teaspoon vanilla
> 2 eggs

8-INCH PIE

In small mixer bowl, combine sugar, butter, chocolate and vanilla. Blend well. Add eggs, one at a time, beating at medium speed for 3 to 5 minutes after each. Pour into baked pastry shell. Chill at least 2 hours. Serve with whipped cream and walnuts if desired.

A summer cooler that heaps big, plump fresh strawberries into mound of almond flavored marshamallow cream.

Strawberry Social Pie

<u>9-inch Graham Cracker Crust</u>, see page 65

> ⅔ cup whipping cream
> ¼ cup light corn syrup
> ¼ teaspoon almond extract
> 2 cups miniature marshmallows
> 1 pint strawberries, sliced (reserve 3 whole
>   strawberries to garnish)

9-INCH PIE

In mixing bowl, beat whipping cream until thick. Gradually add corn syrup; beat until mixture is very stiff. Fold in almond extract and marshmallows. Spread half of whipped cream mixture in graham cracker crust; top with strawberry slices. Cover with remaining whipped cream; garnish with whole strawberries. Chill 5 to 8 hours or overnight.

Tips: 1 packet whipped topping mix may be substituted for whipping cream and corn syrup. Prepare topping mix according to package directions, substituting almond extract for vanilla extract.

If desired, substitute 2 tablespoons curacao liqueur for the almond extract.

A creamy rich filling speckled with morsels of crushed toffee and underlined with mocha-chocolate press in the pan crust.

Toffee Dream Pie

> ¾ cup Pillsbury's Best All Purpose Flour*
> ⅛ teaspoon salt
> ½ teaspoon instant coffee
> 3 tablespoons firmly packed brown sugar
> ½ square (½ oz.) semi-sweet chocolate
> ⅓ cup butter or margarine
> ½ teaspoon vanilla
> 2 tablespoons diced, toasted almonds

<u>Toffee Filling</u>

> 32 (½ lb.) marshmallows
> ⅓ cup milk
> 5 bars (¾ oz. each) chocolate covered
>   toffee candy, crushed
> 1 cup whipping cream

OVEN 375°   8-INCH PIE

In small mixing bowl, combine flour, salt, coffee and sugar. Melt chocolate and butter in small saucepan over low heat; cool slightly. Blend into flour mixture along with vanilla. With floured fingers, press onto bottom and sides of 8-inch pie pan. Bake at 375° for 10 to 12 minutes. Cool. Fill with Toffee Filling. Chill until set; at least 3 hours. Garnish with almonds.

Toffee Filling: Combine marshmallows and milk in top of double boiler. Heat over hot water, stirring occasionally, until marshmallows melt. Remove from heat. Stir in crushed toffee until partially melted. Chill until thickened but not set. Beat cream until thick; fold gently but thoroughly into marshmallow mixture.

*For use with Pillsbury's Best Self-Rising Flour, omit salt.

Brazilian Mocha-Nut Pie

<u>9-inch Baked Pastry Shell</u>, see below

⅓ cup chopped Brazil nuts
I envelope (I tablespoon) unflavored
  gelatin
¼ cup milk
3 egg yolks
I cup milk
½ cup sugar
I tablespoon instant coffee
¼ teaspoon salt
½ teaspoon vanilla
3 egg whites
¼ cup sugar
I cup whipping cream
½ cup chopped Brazil nuts

9-INCH PIE

Prepare pastry shell as directed on page 62 adding ⅓ cup chopped Brazil nuts to flour mixture.

Soften gelatin in ¼ cup milk. In top of double boiler, combine egg yolks, milk, sugar, instant coffee and salt. Beat with rotary beater until well blended. Cook over boiling water, stirring occasionally, until mixture thickens and will coat a metal spoon. Remove from heat. Add vanilla and softened gelatin. Chill until mixture is thick, but not set. In small mixer bowl, beat egg whites until foamy. Gradually add sugar, continuing to beat until stiff, glossy peaks form. Fold into gelatin mixture. In small mixer bowl, beat cream until thick. Fold cream and chopped nuts into gelatin mixture. Spoon filling into baked pastry shell. Chill until firm, 3 to 5 hours.

Date Delight

<u>Date Dessert</u>

I cup Pillsbury's Best All Purpose or
  Self-Rising Flour
½ cup firmly packed brown sugar
½ cup butter or margarine, softened
I egg
½ teaspoon vanilla
¼ cup chopped walnuts
I package (8 oz.) or I¼ cups dates,
  chopped
I cup water
I tablespoon lemon juice
2 cups miniature marshmallows

<u>Whipped Cream Topping</u>

I cup whipping cream
½ cup confectioners' sugar
½ teaspoon vanilla

OVEN 350°   9 TO I2 SERVINGS

Date Dessert: In large mixer bowl, combine flour, brown sugar, butter, egg and vanilla. Blend well at medium speed. Stir in walnuts. Spread in ungreased 9-inch square pan. Bake at 350° for I5 to 20 minutes until light golden brown. In medium saucepan, combine dates, water and lemon juice; bring to boil over medium heat, stirring constantly. Cook until thick. Remove from heat; add marshmallows and stir until partially melted. Spread on baked base. Cool. Top with Whipped Cream Topping. Chill several hours or overnight.

<u>Whipped Cream Topping</u>: In small mixer bowl, beat cream until thick. Add confectioners' sugar and vanilla, blend well.

A three-tiered treat of tangy lime sherbet, crispy macaroon cream and a layer of coconut cream. Make it early and freeze.

Macaroon Crunch Pie

<u>9-inch Baked Pastry Shell</u>, see page 63
  ½ cup toasted coconut
   I pint lime sherbet, softened
1½ cups whipping cream
  ⅓ cup confectioners' sugar
   I cup crushed crisp macaroon cookies
  ½ cup chopped pecans

Sprinkle 6 tablespoons coconut in bottom of baked pastry shell; cover with softened sherbet. In mixing bowl, beat cream with confectioners' sugar until thick; reserve I cup for topping. Fold crushed cookies and pecans into remaining whipped cream; spoon over sherbet, sealing to edge. Garnish with reserved whipped cream and 2 tablespoons coconut. Freeze 6 hours or overnight.

Refreshing as an island breeze is this pineapple chiffon set in a complementary orange-flavored crust. Perfect ending for a summer barbecue.

Pineapple Fluff Pie

Pastry Shell
- 1 cup Pillsbury's Best All Purpose Flour*
- 1 tablespoon sugar
- ½ teaspoon salt
- ⅓ cup shortening
- 1 teaspoon grated orange peel
- 3 tablespoons orange juice or water

Filling
- 1 envelope (1 tablespoon) unflavored gelatin
- 1 can (1 lb. 4 oz.) crushed pineapple, drain and reserve ¼ cup syrup
- ¼ cup sugar
- 2 tablespoons cornstarch
- ½ teaspoon salt
- 3 egg yolks
- 2 cups buttermilk
- 1 tablespoon grated lemon peel
- 2 tablespoons lemon juice
- 3 egg whites
- ¼ cup sugar

OVEN 450°   9-INCH PIE

Pastry Shell: In small mixing bowl, combine flour, sugar and salt. Cut in shortening until particles are the size of small peas. Combine orange peel and juice. Sprinkle over dry ingredients, tossing and stirring lightly with fork. Form into a ball. Flatten to ½-inch thickness; smooth edges. Roll out on floured surface to a circle 1½ inches larger than inverted 9-inch pie pan. Fit loosely into pan. Fold edges to form a rim; flute. Prick generously with fork. Bake at 450° for 8 to 10 minutes, until golden brown. Cool.

Filling: Soften gelatin in reserved pineapple syrup. In saucepan, combine sugar, cornstarch, salt and egg yolks. Stir in buttermilk. Cook over low heat, stirring constantly, until thick. Remove from heat. Add the softened gelatin, lemon peel and lemon juice; mix well. Chill until mixture begins to thicken. Fold in drained pineapple.

In small mixer bowl, beat egg whites until foamy. Gardually add ¼ cup sugar, continuing to beat until stiff, glossy peaks form. Fold into pineapple mixture. Spoon into baked pastry

shell. Chill at least 2 hours before serving.
*For use with Pillsbury's Best Self-Rising Flour, omit salt in pastry.

Walnuts, pressed in a pie-shell, are hidden treasures under the orange chiffon filling, made from frozen orange juice. Garnish with walnuts for a pretty serving.

Orange Fluff Pie

- ¼ cup chopped walnuts
- 9-inch Unbaked Pastry Shell, see page 63
- ½ cup sugar
- 1 envelope (1 tablespoon) unflavored gelatin
- ⅛ teaspoon salt
- 1 cup cold water
- 3 egg yolks, slightly beaten
- ½ cup frozen orange juice concentrate, thawed
- 3 egg whites
- ¼ cup sugar

OVEN 450°   9-INCH PIE

Press walnuts lightly into unbaked pastry shell; prick. Bake at 450° for 8 to 10 minutes until golden brown. Cool.

In medium saucepan, combine sugar, gelatin, salt and water. Cook over medium heat, stirring constantly, until gelatin is dissolved. Remove from heat. Blend a little of the hot mixture into egg yolks; add to hot mixture in saucepan. Cook over low heat, stirring constantly, until mixture coats a metal spoon, about 3 minutes. Remove from heat. Add orange juice. Chill until thickened but not set. Beat egg whites until soft mounds form. Gradually add sugar, beating until stiff peaks form. Fold gently but thoroughly into gelatin mixture. Chill until thickened but not set. Spoon into baked pastry shell. Chill until firm. If desired, serve with whipped cream and garnish with walnuts.

Tip: If desired, a Vanilla Crumb Crust, see page 65, may be used.

Make a cake in a pie pan; split and fill with pineapple, whipped cream and marshmallows — as good as it sounds.

Pineapple Dessert Pie

Cake
> 1¼ cups Pillsbury's Best All Purpose Flour*
> ⅓ cup sugar
> ½ teaspoon soda
> ½ teaspoon salt
> 1 teaspoon vanilla
> ½ cup butter, softened
> 1 egg
> ¼ cup chopped walnuts

Pineapple Filling
> 1 cup whipping cream
> 1 cup miniature marshmallows
> 1 cup (10 oz. jar) pineapple preserves
> 1 teaspoon grated lemon peel

OVEN 325°   6 TO 8 SERVINGS

Cake: In small mixer bowl, combine flour, sugar, soda, salt, vanilla, butter and egg. Blend well at medium speed. Spread in bottom of ungreased 9-inch pie pan. Bake at 325° for 20 to 25 minutes until golden brown. Remove from pan and cool thoroughly. Cut cake in half horizontally to make 2 thin layers. Place bottom layer in pie pan. Spread with half of Pineapple Filling. Top with remaining cake layer and Filling. Sprinkle with walnuts. Chill several hours or overnight.

Pineapple Filling: In small mixer bowl, beat cream until thick. Fold in remaining ingredients.

Self-Rising Flour is not recommended for use in this recipe.

Delicate orange-flavor crust. Inside, sweet rhubarb covered with cream cheese topped with an orangey sour cream. It's as pretty and fresh as spring!

Springtime Cheese Pie

Crust
> 1 cup Pillsbury's Best All Purpose or
>   Self-Rising Flour
> ½ cup butter, softened
> 1 tablespoon sugar
> 1 teaspoon grated orange peel

Rhubarb Filling
> 1 package (1 lb.) frozen rhubarb, slightly
>   thawed
> ½ cup sugar
> ¼ cup Pillsbury's Best All Purpose or
>   Self-Rising Flour

Cream Cheese Filling
> 1 package (8 oz.) cream cheese, softened
> ½ cup sugar
> 1 egg

Topping
> ½ cup dairy sour cream
> 1 tablespoon sugar
> 1 teaspoon grated orange peel

OVEN 425°   9-INCH PIE

Crust: In small mixing bowl, combine all crust ingredients until a dough forms. Press evenly onto bottom and sides of greased 9-inch pie pan. Pour Rhubarb Filling into pastry-lined pan. Bake at 425° for 10 minutes. Remove from oven. Decrease oven temperature to 350°. Pour Cream Cheese Filling over rhubarb. Bake at 350° for 30 to 35 minutes. Spread Topping evenly over pie. Chill several hours or overnight.

Rhubarb Filling: In small mixing bowl, combine all ingredients.

Cream Cheese Filling: In small mixer bowl, combine cream cheese and sugar; beat at medium speed until fluffy. Add egg; beat well.

Topping: In small mixing bowl, combine all ingredients. Blend well.

Tip: For more orange flavor, substitute finely chopped candied orange peel for grated orange peel.

A new twist on cherry dessert. Bright red cherries blanket a creamy lemon layer with a crunchy cookie base above and below. Good for making early and chilling.

Cherry Cream Crunch

    1 cup Pillsbury's Best All Purpose Flour*
 ½ cup firmly packed brown sugar
 ½ cup butter or margarine, softened
 ½ teaspoon salt
 ½ teaspoon cinnamon
    1 teaspoon vanilla
    1 cup flaked or shredded coconut
 ½ cup quick-cooking rolled oats
 ½ cup chopped nuts
    1 can (1 lb. 5 oz.) prepared cherry pie filling

Lemon Filling

    1 can (15 oz.) sweetened condensed milk
    2 eggs
    4 teaspoons grated lemon peel
 ¼ cup lemon juice
 ¼ teaspoon salt

OVEN 375°   9 TO 12 SERVINGS

In large mixer bowl, combine flour, brown sugar, butter, salt, cinnamon and vanilla. Mix at low speed until well blended. Stir in coconut, rolled oats and chopped nuts. Press 2½ cups of crumb mixture in bottom of ungreased 12x8 or 9-inch square pan. Bake at 375° for 12 minutes. Spread with Lemon Filling. Top with cherry pie filling. Sprinkle with remaining crumb mixture. Bake at 375° for 15 to 18 minutes, until lightly browned. Chill thoroughly before serving.

Lemon Filling: In small mixing bowl, combine sweetened condensed milk, eggs, lemon peel, lemon juice and salt. Mix until well blended and slightly thickened.

*For use with Pillsbury's Best Self-Rising Flour, omit salt.

A frozen pie that is frosty pink and cherry-studded. Picture pretty in a flaky sour cream pastry made crunchy with coconut and almonds. An hour to prepare; four hours to freeze.

Party Pink Pie

Pastry
- 1 cup Pillsbury's Best All Purpose Flour*
- ½ teaspoon salt
- ¼ cup flaked coconut
- ⅓ cup shortening
- 2 tablespoons dairy sour cream
- 2 tablespoons cold water
- ¼ cup slivered almonds
- 2 tablespoons flaked coconut

Filling
- 1 package Pillsbury Fluffy White Frosting Mix
- 4 to 5 drops red food coloring
- ½ cup dairy sour cream
- 1 can (1 lb. 5 oz.) prepared cherry pie filling

OVEN 425°   9-INCH PIE

Pastry: In small mixer bowl, combine flour, salt and coconut. Add shortening and mix at low speed until mixture is crumbly. Add sour cream and water; continue mixing at low speed until a dough forms. Shape into a ball. Roll out on floured surface to a circle 1½ inches larger than inverted 9-inch pie pan. Fit loosely into pie pan. Form a rim; flute edge. Prick generously with fork. Bake at 425° for 10 to 12 minutes. Toast remaining coconut and slivered almonds in shallow pan until golden, about 3 minutes.

Filling: Prepare frosting as directed on package; add food coloring. Fold sour cream into 1 cup prepared frosting. Add cherry pie filling to sour cream mixture, blend well. Pour into baked pastry shell. Spread on remaining frosting. Sprinkle with toasted almonds and coconut. Freeze at least 4 hours.

Tip: If desired, fold 2 to 3 tablespoons kirsch into filling.

*For use with Pillsbury's Best Self-Rising Flour, omit salt.

118

A mint-green gelatin cheese cake blanketed with chocolate mint sour cream. Crust can be made easy with sliced refrigerator cookies, too.

Pineapple-Mint Supreme

Cookie Base
   ½ cup Pillsbury's Best All Purpose or
      Self-Rising Flour
   ¼ cup chopped walnuts
   2 tablespoons firmly packed brown sugar
   ¼ cup butter or margarine

Filling
   1 can (1 lb. 4 oz.) crushed pineapple,
      drain and reserve syrup
   1 package (3 oz.) lime-flavored gelatin
   1 package (8 oz.) cream cheese, softened
   1 cup sugar
   ⅔ cup whipping cream
   1 tablespoon lemon juice
   ⅛ teaspoon peppermint extract, if desired

Glaze
   26 solid chocolate mint candy wafers
   ½ cup dairy sour cream or evaporated milk

OVEN 400°   8 TO 10 SERVINGS

Cookie Base: In small mixing bowl, combine flour, walnuts and brown sugar; cut in butter until particles are fine. Press onto bottom of greased 9-inch square pan. Bake at 400° for 5 to 7 minutes until golden brown. Cool. Spoon Filling over cooled base. Chill until set. Top with Glaze, spreading carefully to cover. Chill at least 4 hours or overnight.

Filling: In saucepan, bring reserved pineapple syrup to rolling boil; remove from heat. Add gelatin; stir to dissolve. Stir in drained pineapple. In small mixer bowl, beat cream cheese with sugar until creamy; blend in gelatin mixture. Chill until thickened, but not set. In small mixing bowl, beat whipping cream until thick. Add lemon juice and peppermint extract; continue beating until thick. Fold into cooled pineapple-cheese mixture.

Glaze: In small saucepan, melt candy wafers and sour cream over low heat, stirring constantly.

Tips: Pillsbury Refrigerated Butter Pecan Cookies may be substituted for Cookie Base. Slice cookies ⅛-inch thick, using about half the roll. Line bottom of pan, which has been greased and lightly sugared, with cookie slices,
overlapping slightly. Bake at 375° for 12 to 15 minutes until golden brown.

For lighter dessert, use ⅔ cup partially frozen evaporated milk for whipping cream.

It's easy when you bake the cake and the cheesecake filling all at once. Add sour cream topping and chill.

Cake 'N Cheese Cake

Cake
   1 cup Pillsbury's Best All Purpose Flour*
   ⅔ cup sugar
   1 teaspoon baking powder
   ½ teaspoon salt
   ½ cup butter or margarine, softened
   1 teaspoon vanilla
   1 egg

Cheese Filling
   1 package (8 oz.) cream cheese, softened
   ⅔ cup sugar
   1 cup dairy sour cream
   1 teaspoon vanilla
   3 eggs

Topping
   1 cup dairy sour cream
   ¼ cup sugar
   1 teaspoon vanilla

OVEN 350°   10 TO 12 SERVINGS

Cake: In small mixer bowl, combine all Cake ingredients. Beat at medium speed until well blended. Spread in bottom of greased and floured 9 inch square pan. Pour Cheese Filling over batter. Bake at 350° for 35 to 45 minutes until firm when lightly touched in center. Spread with Topping. Cool; chill at least 4 hours before serving.

Cheese Filling: In small mixer bowl, combine all ingredients. Beat at medium speed until well blended.

Topping: In mixing bowl, combine all ingredients.

*For use with Pillsbury's Best Self-Rising Flour, omit baking powder and salt.

HIGH ALTITUDE ADJUSTMENT — 5,200 FEET. Reduce baking powder to ½ teaspoon.

Pineapple Cheesecake Pie

9-inch Unbaked Pastry Shell, see page 63

   I can (I lb. 5 oz.) prepared pineapple pie filling
   I package (8 oz.) cream cheese, softened
   ½ cup sugar
   ½ teaspoon salt
   ½ cup milk
   I tablespoon lemon juice
   ½ teaspoon vanilla
   2 eggs
   ½ cup chopped pecans

OVEN 375°   9-INCH PIE

Pour pineapple pie filling into unbaked pastry shell with high fluted edge. In small mixer bowl, combine remaining ingredients except pecans. Blend well at medium speed. Pour mixture carefully over pineapple. Sprinkle with pecans. Bake at 375° for 35 to 40 minutes until golden brown. Chill before serving.

Lemon Cheese Pie

8-inch Baked Pastry Shell, see page 63

   I package (8 oz.) cream cheese, softened
   ½ cup sugar
   2 eggs
   I tablespoon lemon juice
   I teaspoon grated lemon peel
   I teaspoon vanilla

OVEN 350°   8-INCH PIE

In small mixer bowl, combine all ingredients. Blend well at medium speed. Pour into baked pastry shell. Bake at 350° for 20 to 25 minutes until slightly firm in center. Cool. Chill thoroughly before serving. If desired, serve with whipped cream.

Tip: Refrigerated Slice and Bake Cookie Crust, see page 65 may be used in place of pastry shell.

Date Cream Roll

Date Roll

   5 egg yolks
   ⅔ cup Pillsbury's Best All Purpose Flour*
   ½ cup sugar
   I tablespoon instant coffee
   2 tablespoons water
   I package (8 oz.) or 1¼ cups chopped dates
   ½ cup chopped almonds
   5 egg whites
   ¼ teaspoon salt
   ¼ teaspoon cream of tartar
   ¼ cup sugar
   Confectioners' sugar

Coffee Filling

   I cup whipping cream
   3 tablespoons sugar
   2 teaspoons instant coffee

OVEN 350°   8 TO 10 SERVINGS

Date Roll: In small mixer bowl, combine egg yolks, flour, ½ cup sugar, instant coffee and water. Blend well at medium speed. Stir in dates and almonds. In large mixer bowl, combine egg whites, salt and cream of tartar. Beat at high speed until soft mounds form. Gradually add ¼ cup sugar; continue beating until stiff peaks form. Fold egg yolk mixture gently but thoroughly into egg whites. Spread in 15x10-inch jelly roll pan, greased, lined with waxed paper, then greased again. Bake at 350° for 20 to 25 minutes until cake springs back when touched lightly in center. Turn out immediately onto towel sprinkled with confectioners' sugar. Remove paper. Roll in towel, starting with 10-inch end. Cool. Unroll and spread with Coffee Filling. Roll again. Sprinkle confectioners' sugar over top. Chill thoroughly. Slice with a very sharp knife.

Coffee Filling: In small mixer bowl, combine all ingredients and beat until thick.

Tip: If desired, fold 2 to 3 tablespoons brandy into Coffee Filling.

*For use with Pillsbury's Best Self-Rising Flour, omit salt.

Make a sponge cake go fancy! Start with ready-made or your favorite sponge cake. Surround slices with luscious orange cream and chill.

Orange-Filled Sponge Dessert

   1 cup sugar
   3 tablespoons cornstarch
   ¼ teaspoon salt
   1½ cups water
   ½ cup orange juice
   2 tablespoons lemon juice
   1 egg, slightly beaten
   1 tablespoon butter or margarine
   1 tablespoon grated orange peel
   1 teaspoon grated lemon peel
   ½ cup whipping cream
   1 cup cut-up orange sections
   1 sponge or egg custard angel food
     loaf cake

6 TO 8 SERVINGS

In saucepan, combine sugar, cornstarch, and salt. Add water, orange juice, lemon juice and egg; mix well. Cook over medium heat, stirring constantly, until very thick. Add butter, orange peel and lemon peel. Cool. Beat whipping cream until thick; fold into cooked mixture along with orange sections. Cut loaf cake into ½-inch slices. Line bottom of 8-inch square pan with half of slices; cover with half of filling. Cover with more cake slices and remaining filling. Chill several hours or overnight. To serve, cut into squares. If desired, garnish with additional whipped cream and orange slices.

Tips: Any leftover cake may be used for a quick dessert by topping with fresh fruit and whipped cream.

Drained, cut-up mandarin oranges may be used for orange sections.

The cherries are under the cheesecake in this butter-crust chilled pie. The crust is press-in-the-pan easy. Pretty to serve, and only an hour to prepare, but be sure to allow time to chill.

Cheesecake Cherry Pie

   1 cup Pillsbury's Best All Purpose Flour*
   2 tablespoons sugar
   ⅛ teaspoon salt
   ½ cup butter or margarine, softened
   1 can (1 lb. 5 oz.) prepared cherry pie
     filling

Cheesecake Topping
   2 packages (3 oz. each) cream cheese,
     softened
   1 egg
   ⅓ cup sugar
   ½ teaspoon vanilla

OVEN 350°   9-INCH PIE

In small mixer bowl, combine flour, sugar and salt. Cut in butter, using low speed of mixer, until mixture is crumbly. Press into bottom and up sides of 9-inch pie pan. Pour cherry pie filling over crust. Spoon on Cheesecake Topping. Bake at 350° for 30 to 35 minutes until topping is firm. Chill thoroughly before serving.

Cheesecake Topping: In small mixer bowl, combine all ingredients. Beat at high speed until well blended.

*For use with Pillsbury's Best Self-Rising Flour, omit salt in crust.

Sponge cake (that you buy or make yourself) sliced and layered with apricot preserves and custard sauce. Assemble early for the buffet or church supper.

Sponge Custard Delight

Cake

    4 egg whites
    ½ teaspoon cream of tartar
    ½ teaspoon salt
    ⅓ cup sugar
    1 cup Pillsbury's Best All Purpose Flour*
    ¾ cup sugar
    1 teaspoon baking powder
    4 egg yolks
    ¼ cup water
    1 teaspoon grated lemon peel
    2 tablespoons lemon juice
    1 cup (10 oz. jar) apricot preserves

Custard

    1 cup sugar
    ¼ cup cornstarch
    ⅛ teaspoon salt
    2 egg yolks
    1 can (14½ oz.) or 1⅔ cups evaporated milk
    1⅔ cups water
    2 egg whites
    2 teaspoons vanilla

OVEN 350°   9 TO 12 SERVINGS

Cake: In large mixer bowl, combine egg whites, cream of tartar and salt. Beat at high speed until soft peaks form. Gradually add ⅓ cup sugar, beating until very stiff peaks form. Do not underbeat. In small mixer bowl, combine flour, ¾ cup sugar, baking powder, egg yolks, water, lemon peel and lemon juice at medium speed; beat 1 minute. Fold gently into egg whites. Pour into ungreased 9 or 10-inch tube pan. Bake at 350° for 30 to 40 minutes until cake springs back when touched lightly in center. Invert immediately. Cool thoroughly. Cut cake into ½-inch slices. Pour ½ cup Custard into bottom of 13x9-inch baking dish or 3-quart casserole. Place a layer of cake slices over Custard. Spread each piece with apricot preserves. Cover with Custard. Repeat layers, ending with Custard. Garnish with maraschino cherries, if desired. Chill thoroughly.

Custard: In top of double boiler, combine sugar, cornstarch, salt and egg yolks. Gradually add milk and water; stir until blended. Beat egg whites until stiff but not dry. Fold into milk mixture. Cook over boiling water, stirring constantly, until mixture is slightly thick and coats a spoon. Remove from heat; add vanilla.

Tips: Timesaver—buy the cake and prepare Custard. Put together as directed.

This is an excellent make-ahead dessert for buffet dinner or a dessert party.

*For use with Pillsbury's Best Self-Rising Flour, omit salt and baking powder in Cake.

A gelatin-cream filling of sweet dark cherries sets cool and light in a vanilla cookie crust. You can add a special spark with brandy, if you wish.

Cherry Fluff Pie

9-inch Baked Vanilla Crumb Crust, see page 65

    1 can (1 lb.) dark sweet pitted cherries, drain and reserve syrup
    1 teaspoon lemon juice
    1 package (3 oz.) black cherry flavored gelatin
    ⅓ cup chopped walnuts
    ½ teaspoon almond extract
    1 cup whipping cream
    ½ cup confectioners' sugar

9-INCH PIE

Combine reserved cherry syrup and enough water to measure 1¼ cups. Bring to boil in medium saucepan. Remove from heat. Add lemon juice and gelatin; stir until dissolved. Chill until thickened, but not set. In small mixer bowl, beat thickened gelatin mixture at high speed until fluffy. Fold in cherries, walnuts and almond extract. Beat cream with confectioners' sugar until thick. Fold into cherry mixture. Spoon into baked vanilla crumb crust. Chill until firm, at least 2 hours.

Tips: 2 to 3 tablespoons brandy or kirsch may be folded in with the whipped cream.

Filling may be spooned into 9-inch baked pastry shell.

A light and airy chocolate and vanilla layered chilled cheesecake with crushed mint candy in the crust and on the top.

Neopolitan Cheesecake

Crust

 1 cup Pillsbury's Best All Purpose Flour*
 ½ cup coarsely crushed after dinner mints
 1 teaspoon vanilla
 ½ cup butter or margarine

Neopolitan Filling

 ⅓ cup sugar
 ¼ teaspoon salt
 1 envelope (1 tablespoon) unflavored
  gelatin
 ¾ cup milk
 2 egg yolks, slightly beaten
 1 package (8 oz.) cream cheese
 2 egg whites
 1 teaspoon vanilla
 ¼ cup sugar
 1 cup whipping cream
 1 cup (6 oz. package) semi-sweet
  chocolate pieces, melted
 2 tablespoons crushed after dinner mints

OVEN 400°   9 SERVINGS

Crust: In small mixer bowl, combine flour, candy and vanilla. Cut in butter, using low speed of mixer until mixture is crumbly. Press into bottom of 9-inch square pan. Bake at 400° for 12 to 15 minutes or until delicately browned. Cool.

Neopolitan Filling: In saucepan, combine ⅓ cup sugar, salt and gelatin. Add milk and slightly beaten egg yolks. Cook over medium heat, stirring constantly, until mixture comes to a boil. Remove from heat. Add cream cheese; allow to soften, then beat with rotary beater until smooth. Cool until slightly thickened. In small mixer bowl, combine egg whites and vanilla. Beat at high speed until foamy. Add sugar gradually, continuing to beat until stiff, glossy peaks form. Fold into gelatin mixture. Beat cream until thick. Fold into gelatin mixture. Divide in half. Pour melted chocolate into one portion. Spoon into baked crust. Spoon vanilla filling over chocolate. Sprinkle on crushed candy after dinner mints. Chill at least 2 hours before serving.

*For use with Pillsbury's Best Self-Rising Flour, use unsalted butter in crust.

It's a jelly roll, but the news is in the filling: a perfect combination of chocolate and mint. Make ahead and chill.

Chocolate Fluff Roll

Cake

4 egg whites
½ cup sugar
4 egg yolks
¼ cup sugar
2 tablespoons water
1 teaspoon vanilla
⅔ cup Pillsbury's Best All Purpose Flour*
1 teaspoon baking powder
½ teaspoon salt

Chocolate Mint Cream Filling

½ cup sugar
¼ cup cocoa
⅛ teaspoon salt
½ teaspoon vanilla
1½ cups whipping cream
¼ cup white creme de menthe

OVEN 375°   8 TO 10 SERVINGS

Cake: In large mixer bowl, beat egg whites at high speed until soft mounds form. Gradually add ½ cup sugar, beating until stiff peaks form. Set aside. In small mixer bowl, combine egg yolks, ¼ cup sugar, water and vanilla; beat until thick and lemon colored. Fold egg yolk mixture gently into egg whites. Combine the dry ingredients; add half at a time, folding gently after each addition until all dry particles disappear. Spread in 15x10-inch jelly roll pan, greased, lined with waxed paper, greased again and floured lightly. Bake at 375° for 12 to 15 minutes, until top springs back when touched lightly in center. Turn out immediately onto towel sprinkled with confectioners' sugar. Remove paper. Roll cake in towel, starting with 10-inch side. Cool. Unroll and spread with Chocolate Mint Cream Filling. Roll again. Place on serving plate, seam side down. Sprinkle confectioners' sugar on top of cake. Chill several hours before serving.

Chocolate Mint Cream Filling: In small mixer bowl, combine sugar, cocoa, salt, vanilla and whipping cream. Beat until thick; fold in creme de menthe.

*For use with Pillsbury's Best Self-Rising Flour, omit baking powder and salt in Cake.

Frilly and fun to make. Fill a jelly roll with light pumpkin filling and freeze. Make it easy with pumpkin ice cream.

Frosty Pumpkin Creme Log

    5 eggs
    I cup sugar
    I½ teaspoons vanilla
    I cup Pillsbury's Best All Purpose Flour*
    I teaspoon baking powder
    I teaspoon salt
    I teaspoon cinnamon
    ½ teaspoon nutmeg
    Confectioners' sugar

Filling

    I cup milk
    I package (8 oz.) or 32 marshmallows
    I cup cooked or canned pumpkin
    ¼ cup firmly packed brown sugar
    I teaspoon cinnamon
    I teaspoon vanilla
    ½ teaspoon salt
    I cup whipping cream

OVEN 400°   16 TO 18 SERVINGS

In large mixer bowl, beat eggs at high speed until foamy. Gradually add sugar; beat until thick and ivory colored. Blend in vanilla. Combine flour, baking powder, salt, cinnamon and nutmeg; fold into eggs gently but thoroughly. Spread in 15x10-inch jelly roll pan that has been greased, lined with waxed paper and greased again. Bake at 400° for 12 to 15 minutes until cake springs back when touched lightly in center. Cool 5 minutes. Turn out onto aluminum foil heavily sprinkled with confectioners' sugar. Remove waxed paper. Roll loosely in foil, starting with 15-inch side. Cool. Unroll and spread partially frozen Filling down center. Bring 15-inch sides together so they just meet. Wrap in the foil. Freeze 4 to 6 hours or overnight.

Filling: In saucepan, combine milk and marshmallows; cook over medium heat, stirring occasionally, until marshmallows melt. Stir in pumpkin, brown sugar, cinnamon, vanilla and salt. Chill until thick. Beat cream until thick.

Fold into pumpkin mixture. Freeze, stirring occasionally, until mixture is partially frozen and holds shape.

Tip: I½ quarts pumpkin ice cream, softened, may be substituted for Filling.

*For use with Pillsbury's Best Self-Rising Flour, omit baking powder and salt.

Frothy golden butterscotch studded with nuts. A refrigerator dessert you can do early. For variety try a cookie crumb crust.

Butterscotch Nut Chiffon Pie

9-inch Baked Pastry Shell, see page 63

    I envelope (I tablespoon) unflavored
      gelatin
    ¼ cup cold water
    3 egg yolks
    I cup milk
    I cup firmly packed brown sugar
    ½ teaspoon salt
    3 egg whites
    ¼ cup firmly packed brown sugar
    ½ cup whipping cream
    ½ cup chopped nuts

9-INCH PIE

Soften gelatin in cold water. In top of double boiler, combine egg yolks, milk, brown sugar and salt. Beat with rotary beater until blended. Cook over hot water, stirring occasionally, until mixture will coat a spoon, 25 to 30 minutes. Add softened gelatin; stir until dissolved. Chill, stirring occasionally, until thickened, but not set. In small mixer bowl, beat egg whites at high speed until foamy. Gradually add brown sugar, continuing to beat until stiff, glossy peaks form. In small mixing bowl, beat cream until thick. Fold beaten egg whites, whipped cream and chopped nuts into gelatin mixture. Spoon into baked pastry shell. Chill until firm. Garnish with whipped cream, if desired.

Conversation Piece Pies And Desserts

● The topic is sure to be your extraordinary dessert: foreign or flaming, multi-layered and magnificent; a dessert with a new idea, a new look or a strong appeal to children. The desserts in this chapter run the gamut from cheesecakes, layered wonders, blitz tortes and foreign specialties to creative "fun" desserts that end your meal with flair and surprise.

Tangy raspberry and butter cream fillings are the center of attention between split yellow cake layers. As good-tasting as it is pretty . . . served in whipped cream-topped squares or wedges.

Raspberry Continental

    1 package Pillsbury One Layer Size Yellow
       Batter Cake Mix
       Chopped walnuts

<u>Butter Filling</u>
    1½ cups confectioners' sugar
    ½ cup butter, softened

<u>Raspberry Filling</u>
    ¼ cup sugar
    2 tablespoons cornstarch
    1 package (10 oz.) frozen raspberries,
       thawed, undrained

<u>Whipped Cream Topping</u>
    ½ cup whipping cream
    2 tablespoons sugar

OVEN 350°   9 SERVINGS

Prepare and bake cake mix in 8 or 9-inch round layer or square pan as directed on package. Cool thoroughly. Cut in half horizontally with a very sharp knife to make 2 layers. Place bottom layer on serving plate. Spread with Butter Filling, then Raspberry Filling. Top with other layer of cake, then Whipped Cream Topping. Sprinkle with chopped walnuts. Chill several hours or overnight.

<u>Butter Filling</u>: In small mixer bowl, gradually add confectioners' sugar to butter; cream well.

<u>Raspberry Filling</u>: In small saucepan, combine sugar and cornstarch. Add raspberries. Cook over medium heat, stirring constantly, until thick and clear. Cool completely.

<u>Whipped Cream Topping</u>: Beat cream until thick. Blend in sugar.

<u>Tip:</u> *If desired, add 1 egg to Butter Filling. Beat until fluffy.*

HIGH ALTITUDE ADJUSTMENT — Follow cake mix package recommendations.

A layered triumph, with whipped cream center. Cake and frosting mixes bake together, studded with chocolate bits and pecans. Make early and chill.

"Sweet-Dreams" Cream Torte

     1 package Pillsbury Yellow Batter
       Cake Mix
 ½ cup semi-sweet chocolate pieces
 ½ cup chopped pecans
     1 package Pillsbury Fluffy White
       Frosting Mix
     1 tablespoon sugar
 ⅛ teaspoon cinnamon

Filling
 ¾ cup whipping cream
     3 tablespoons confectioners' sugar
 ½ teaspoon vanilla

OVEN 350°   12 TO 16 SERVINGS

Grease and flour bottoms and sides of two 9-inch round layer pans. Fit a 15x3-inch strip of aluminum foil across bottom and up sides of each pan, allowing to extend beyond edges of pan; fold ends over edges of pans. Prepare cake mix as directed on package. Pour batter into prepared pans. Sprinkle with chocolate pieces and pecans. Prepare Frosting Mix as directed on package; spread over chocolate and nuts, sealing to edges. Combine sugar and cinnamon; sprinkle over frosting. Bake at 350° for 35 to 40 minutes until toothpick inserted in center comes out clean. Cool 10 minutes. Loosen edges; lift out of pan with foil. Remove foil. Cool completely. Stack layers, bottoms together, spreading Filling between. Chill until serving time.

Filling: In small mixing bowl, beat whipping cream with confectioners' sugar until thick. Blend in vanilla.

HIGH ALTITUDE ADJUSTMENT — Follow cake mix package recommendations.

Bridge club beauty! Giant eight-inch cookies are layered with chocolate pudding made light with whipped cream. Do it ahead.

Easy Cookie Dessert

Cookie
 1½ cups Pillsbury's Best All Purpose Flour*
 ¾ cup sugar
 ½ teaspoon baking powder
 ¼ teaspoon salt
 ½ cup butter or margarine, softened
     1 teaspoon vanilla
     1 egg

Chocolate Filling
     1 package (4 oz.) chocolate pudding and
       pie filling mix
 ½ cup whipping cream
 ½ teaspoon rum flavoring

OVEN 375°   12 SERVINGS

Cookie: In large mixer bowl, combine all Cookie ingredients; blend well at medium speed. Divide batter into 4 parts by spreading onto bottom of four 8-inch round layer pans, well greased and lined with waxed paper on the bottom. Bake at 375° for 8 to 10 minutes until light brown around the edges. Cool slightly; remove from pans. Cool thoroughly. Place a baked layer onto serving plate. Spread with one-fourth of Chocolate Filling; top with another layer. Continue to spread Chocolate Filling and stack layers, ending with Filling. Chill several hours before serving.

Chocolate Filling: Prepare chocolate pudding and pie filling according to package directions. Cool. Beat cream until thick; fold into pudding along with rum flavoring.

Tip: If you have only two round layer pans, bake half of dough, covering remainder. After first layers are baked and out of pans, bake second half of dough.

*Self-Rising Flour in not recommended for use in this recipe.

127

A chocolate-crusted cheesecake, drizzled with chocolate and topped further with sour cream. The tip for the substitute cookie crust can save you time and effort.

Chocolate Ripple Cheese Torte

1¼ cups Pillsbury's Best All Purpose Flour*
¼ cup firmly packed brown sugar
½ cup butter or margarine
½ cup chopped pecans
½ cup semi-sweet chocolate pieces
2 tablespoons milk

Filling

2 packages (8 oz. each) cream cheese, softened
3 egg yolks
¾ cup sugar
1 teaspoon vanilla
3 egg whites

Topping

1 cup dairy sour cream
2 tablespoons sugar
1 teaspoon vanilla

OVEN 350°   12 TO 16 SERVINGS

In small mixing bowl, combine flour and brown sugar; cut in butter until particles are fine. Stir in pecans. Press firmly onto bottom of greased 9-inch square pan. Bake at 350° for 10 to 12 minutes until lightly browned. Spread Filling over base. Melt chocolate pieces with milk over low heat; drizzle over Filling. Bake at 325° for 45 minutes or until set. Spread with Topping. Return to oven for 5 minutes more. Cool completely. Chill.

Filling: In large mixer bowl, beat cream cheese until smooth. Add egg yolks; beat well. Gradually add sugar and vanilla; mix thoroughly. Beat egg whites until stiff, but not dry. Fold into cream cheese mixture.

Topping: In small mixing bowl, combine all ingredients; blend well.

Tip: Pillsbury Refrigerated Butter Pecan Cookies may be substituted for cookie crust. Slice cookie dough ⅛ inch thick, using about half the roll. Line bottom of pan which has been greased and lightly sugared, with cookie slices, overlapping slightly. Bake and continue as directed above.

*Not recommended for use with Pillsbury's Best Self-Rising Flour.

Refrigerated cookie slices serve as the bottom crust of this delicious cheese cake for chocolate lovers. Make ahead for a special occasion.

Swiss Chocolate Cheese Cake

Cookie Crust

1 cup Pillsbury's Best All Purpose Flour*
¼ cup sugar
¼ teaspoon salt
⅓ cup butter

Filling

1 package (8 oz.) cream cheese
2 squares (1 oz. each) unsweetened chocolate, melted
2 eggs
⅔ cup sugar
2 tablespoons flour
¼ teaspoon salt
⅔ cup light cream
½ cup chopped shredded or flaked coconut, if desired
1 teaspoon vanilla

OVEN 350°   10 TO 12 SERVINGS

Cookie Crust: In small mixing bowl, combine flour, sugar and salt; cut in butter until particles are fine. Press crumb mixture onto bottom of greased 8-inch square pan. Cover with Filling. Bake at 350° for 40 to 45 minutes until firm. Chill at least 2 hours before serving.

Filling: In small mixer bowl, beat cream cheese with chocolate at medium speed until smooth and creamy. Add eggs; beat well. Blend in sugar, flour and salt; mix well. Stir in cream, coconut and vanilla.

Tip: Pillsbury Refrigerated Sugar Cookies may be substituted for Cookie Crust. Slice cookies ⅛-inch thick, using about half the roll. Line bottom of pan, which has been greased and lightly sugared, with cookie slices, overlapping slightly.

*For use with Pillsbury's Best Self-Rising Flour, omit salt in Cookie Crust.

Sixteen gorgeous servings of this six-layer beauty. Flaky butter pastry rounds alternated with vanilla pudding and luscious raspberry filling. Prepare everything early, then assemble 2 hours before serving.

Raspberry Ribbon Torte

Pastry
   2 cups Pillsbury's Best All Purpose Flour*
   ¼ teaspoon salt
   1 cup butter or margarine, softened
   4 to 6 tablespoons water
   Sugar

Vanilla Filling
   1 package (3¾ oz.) instant vanilla
      pudding mix
   1½ cups milk

Raspberry Filling
   2 tablespoons cornstarch
   ¼ cup water
   1 package (10 oz.) frozen raspberries,
      thawed and undrained

Topping
   1 cup whipping cream
   ⅓ cup sugar
   ¼ teaspoon almond extract

OVEN 450°   16 SERVINGS

Pastry: In large mixing bowl, combine flour and salt. Cut in butter until particles are the size of small peas. Add water, a little at a time, tossing and stirring lightly with fork. Form into a ball; divide into six equal portions. Roll out each portion on floured surface to a 9-inch circle; cut around an inverted 9-inch pie pan to even edges. Transfer each circle to a cool baking sheet. Prick generously with fork; sprinkle each with about 1½ teaspoons sugar. Bake at 450° for 5 to 7 minutes, until golden brown. Remove from cookie sheet. Cool thoroughly. Within 2 hours of serving time, stack layers, spreading Vanilla and Raspberry Fillings alternately between layers, ending with Raspberry layer on top. Spread Topping on sides and around top edge of Torte. Serve within 2 hours.

Vanilla Filling: In small mixing bowl, combine instant pudding mix and milk. Prepare as directed on package. Chill thoroughly.

Raspberry Filling: In small saucepan, combine cornstarch and water; add raspberries with syrup. Cook over medium heat, stirring constantly, until thick. Cool.

Topping: In small mixing bowl, combine Topping ingredients. Beat until thickened.

*For use with Pillsbury's Best Self-Rising Flour, omit salt in Pastry.

Pears and chocolate mints—all baked under a golden butter topping. An easy and unusual combination.

Pear-adise Chocolate Dessert

> I can (I lb. I3 oz.) pear halves, drained
> 8 solid chocolate mint candy wafers
> ¾ cup orange juice
> I½ cups Pillsbury's Best All Purpose Flour*
> I cup sugar
> ¼ teaspoon salt
> I tablespoon grated orange peel
> I cup butter or margarine

OVEN 375°   8 SERVINGS

Arrange pear halves, cut-side up in greased 8-inch square pan. Place one mint wafer in hollow of each; pour on orange juice. In large mixing bowl, combine flour, sugar, salt and orange peel. Cut in butter until particles are the size of small peas. Sprinkle mixture over fruit. Bake at 375° for 40 to 45 minutes until golden brown. Serve warm or cold with whipped cream.

Tip: 4 fresh pears, peeled and cut in half, may be used.

*For use with Pillsbury's Best Self-Rising Flour, omit salt.

A new look to an old favorite. Individual Alaskas with surprises of pastry rounds, pineapple and sherbet hidden under clouds of fluffy frosting. Prepare early and freeze.

Hawaiian Alaska

> I cup Pilllsbury's Best All Purpose Flour*
> ½ teaspoon salt
> ⅓ cup shortening
> 3 to 4 tablespoons water
> I package Pillsbury Fluffy White
>   Frosting Mix
> 5 slices pineapple, well-drained
> I pint pineapple sherbet

OVEN 450°   5 SERVINGS

In small mixing bowl, combine flour and salt; cut in shortening until mixture is the size of small peas. Sprinkle water, a little at a time, over mixture, while tossing and stirring lightly with fork. Add water to driest particles, pushing lumps to side, until dough is just moist enough to hold together. Form into a ball. Flatten to ½ inch thickness; smooth edges. Roll out on floured surface to ⅛ inch thickness. Cut into 5 rounds, 4 inches in diameter. Place on ungreased cookie sheet; prick with fork. Bake at 450° for 8 to I0 minutes until golden brown. Cool completely on cookie sheet. Prepare Frosting Mix as directed on package. Top each pastry round with pineapple slice; then scoop of sherbet. Cover each with frosting sealing to cookie sheet and completely covering sherbet. Freeze at least 3 hours or until serving time. Bake at 500° for 5 minutes until lightly browned. Serve immediately.

*For use with Pillsbury's Best Self-Rising Flour, omit salt.

Curry lovers—an interesting finish or accompaniment to a special meal. Mixed fruits with a baked-on crunchy curry topping.

Baked Fruit Curry

> I can (I lb. I3 oz.) peach halves, drained
> I can (I lb.) pear halves, drained
> I can (I lb. 4½ oz.) pineapple spears,
>   drained
> 2 tablespoons chopped crystallized ginger,
>   if desired
> I cup Pillsbury's Best All Purpose
>   or Self-Rising Flour
> I cup firmly packed brown sugar
> I teaspoon curry powder
> ½ cup butter or margarine

OVEN 375°   6 SERVINGS

Arrange fruits in greased 8-inch square pan; sprinkle on ginger. In mixing bowl, combine flour, brown sugar and curry powder. Cut in butter until mixture is crumbly. Sprinkle over fruit. Bake at 375° for 20 to 25 minutes until light golden brown. Serve warm or cold, with whipped cream, if desired.

Tips: May be served as meat accompaniment. This has a definite curry flavor. If desired, reduce the amount of curry powder to suit your taste.

An elegant, three-layer blitz-torte with raspberry, coconut meringue and sour cream layers throughout . . . all chilled.

Sunday Special Torte

Cake
2 cups Pillsbury's Best All Purpose Flour*
½ cup sugar
½ teaspoon baking powder
½ teaspoon salt
1 cup butter or margarine, softened
2 tablespoons milk
1 teaspoon vanilla
5 egg yolks
1 jar (8 or 10 oz.) or ¾ cup raspberry
   preserves
2 cups dairy sour cream

Meringue
5 egg whites
¼ teaspoon salt
1 cup sugar
1 can (3½ oz.) or 1⅓ cups flaked coconut
1 teaspoon vanilla

OVEN 350°   12 TO 14 SERVINGS

Cake: In large mixer bowl, combine all Cake ingredients, except raspberry preserves and sour cream. Mix at low speed 3 minutes, until well blended. Spread batter in 3 greased 9-inch round layer pans. Spread raspberry preserves over batter. Spread Meringue over preserves. Bake at 350° for 35 to 40 minutes, until light golden brown. Cool 15 minutes; remove from pans. Turn cakes, meringue-side-up. Cool completely. Stack layers, meringue side up, spreading sour cream between layers and leaving meringue top plain. Chill several hours or overnight.

Meringue: In small mixer bowl, combine egg whites and salt. Beat at high speed until foamy. Gradually add sugar, continuing to beat until stiff, glossy peaks form. Fold in coconut and vanilla.

Tip: If you don't have three 9-inch layer pans, hold ⅓ of dough and toppings in refrigerator. Bake as soon as pan is available.

*For use with Pillsbury's Best Self-Rising Flour, omit baking powder and salt.

Ingredients from the dairy case, including the crust of sliced refrigerated cookie dough. Golden cheesecake filling with the hint of lemon. Two hours and chill.

Cookie-Crust Cheese Cake

1 cup Pillsbury's Best All Purpose Flour*
2 tablespoons sugar
½ teaspoon baking powder
¼ teaspoon salt
⅓ cup butter or margarine
1 egg, beaten

Filling
4 egg whites
½ cup sugar
4 packages (3 oz. each) cream cheese,
   softened
½ cup sugar
2 tablespoons flour
¼ teaspoon salt
4 egg yolks
1 tablespoon grated lemon peel
1 tablespoon lemon juice
1 cup dairy sour cream

OVEN 325°   10 TO 12 SERVINGS

In small mixing bowl, combine flour, sugar, baking powder and salt. Cut in butter until particles are fine. Add egg; mix until dough is moist enough to hold together. Pat into bottom of 9-inch springform pan. Cover with Filling. Bake at 325° for 1 hour until lightly browned. Turn off heat; leave in oven for ½ hour. Cool. Chill completely before serving.

Filling: In large mixer bowl, beat egg whites at high speed until soft mounds form. Gradually add ½ cup sugar; continue beating until stiff, glossy peaks form. Set aside. In small mixer bowl, combine cream cheese, ½ cup sugar, flour and salt; blend well. Add egg yolks, lemon peel, lemon juice and sour cream; beat until light and creamy. Fold in egg whites gently but thoroughly.

Tip: Pillsbury Refrigerated Sugar Cookies may be substituted for crust. Slice cookie dough ⅛-inch thick, using about half the roll. Line bottom of pan, which has been greased and lightly sugared, with cookie slices, overlapping slightly. Bake at 375° for 8 to 10 minutes until lightly browned. Cover with Filling and proceed as directed.

*For use with Pillsbury's Best Self-Rising Flour, omit baking powder and salt in cookie crust.

Creamy peach filling nestles between two spongy layers of cake. Topped off with whipped cream and coconut.

Heavenly Peach Fancy

Cake
    4 eggs
    I teaspoon vanilla
    I cup sugar
    I cup Pillsbury's Best All Purpose Flour*
    I teaspoon baking powder
    ¼ teaspoon salt
    ⅓ cup butter or margarine, melted
    2 tablespoons milk
    ½ cup toasted coconut

Filling
    I can (15 oz.) sweetened condensed milk
    ¼ cup lemon juice
    I can (I lb. 14 oz.) or 2 cups peach
      slices, drained and diced

Topping
    I cup whipping cream
    2 tablespoons sugar
    ¼ teaspoon vanilla

OVEN 375°   6 TO 8 SERVINGS

<u>Cake:</u> In large mixer bowl, beat eggs with vanilla at high speed until foamy. Gradually add sugar; continue beating until thick and ivory colored. Do not underbeat. Combine flour, baking powder and salt; fold into egg mixture gently, but thoroughly. Combine melted butter and milk, fold gently into batter. Spread in 15x10-inch jelly roll pan, greased on bottom, lined with waxed paper and greased again. Bake at 375° for 15 to 20 minutes until cake springs back when lightly touched in center. Loosen edges and turn out immediately onto wire rack. Remove paper. Cool. Cut in half crosswise to make two 10x7½-inch layers. Stack layers, spreading filling between; top with Topping. Sprinkle with toasted coconut. Chill at least 2 hours.

<u>Filling:</u> In small mixing bowl, combine condensed milk and lemon juice; stir until thickened. Fold in peaches; chill until of spreading consistency.

<u>Topping:</u> In small mixing bowl, combine all ingredients; beat until thick.

*For use with Pillsbury's Best Self-Rising Flour, omit baking powder and salt.

Old world richness in this warm-from-the-oven dessert. Apple baked inside a rich butter pastry roll. Preserves add a final glaze.

Viennese Apple Pastry
    1⅓ cups Pillsbury's Best All Purpose
      Flour*
    ½ teaspoon salt
    ½ cup butter or margarine
    4 to 5 tablespoons cold water
    I cup peeled, thinly sliced apples
    3 tablespoons sugar
    I tablespoon flour
    2 tablespoons sliced almonds
    3 tablespoons apricot or peach preserves

OVEN 450°   6 SERVINGS

In small mixing bowl, combine flour and salt. Cut in butter until mixture is size of small peas. Sprinkle water, a little at a time, over mixture while stirring with fork until dough is just moist enough to hold together. Roll out on floured surface to 12-inch square. Place on ungreased cookie sheet. Toss apple slices with sugar and I tablespoon flour. Place slices down center of dough. Fold up about ½ inch at each end. Fold sides over apples, leaving an inch of apples showing down center. Sprinkle with almonds. Bake at 450° for 15 to 20 minutes until golden brown. Spread immediately with preserves. Serve warm or cold, cut in slices.

*Self-Rising Flour is not recommended for use in this recipe.

A bright idea for your next pint of fresh strawberries: A glazed cream puff ring with sliced strawberries and cream filling. Fill another time with whipped cream and another fruit.

Strawberry Puff Ring

6 tablespoons butter or margarine
¾ cup hot water
¾ cup Pillsbury's Best All Purpose Flour*
½ teaspoon salt
3 eggs
1 pint fresh strawberries, sliced and chilled (reserve 3 or 4 nice, whole berries to garnish)

Cream Filling

1 package (3¼ oz.) vanilla pudding and pie filling mix
2 cups milk

Glaze

1 cup confectioners' sugar
2 to 3 tablespoons warm water

OVEN 425°   8 TO 10 SERVINGS

In saucepan, combine butter and water; bring to a boil. Add flour and salt all at once; cook over medium heat, stirring constantly until mixture leaves sides of pan in smooth compact ball, about 2 minutes. Cool 1 minute. Add eggs, one at a time, beating vigorously after each until mixture is smooth and glossy. Spoon dough in ring shape, about 8 inches in diameter on greased cookie sheet. Bake at 425° for 30 to 35 minutes until golden brown. Turn off oven. Prick puff with sharp knife. Leave puff in oven 20 minutes to dry out center. Cool; slice off top of ring. Spoon Cream Filling into bottom half of ring. Top with fresh berries. Replace top and drizzle with glaze; garnish with reserved whole strawberries.

Cream Filling: In saucepan, combine pudding mix and milk; mix well. Cook over medium heat, stirring constantly until mixture thickens and boils. Cover and cool. Chill completely, 1 or 2 hours.

Glaze: In small mixing bowl, combine confectioners' sugar and water; mix until smooth.

Tip: 1 package (3¾ oz.) instant vanilla pudding and pie filling mix may be used for filling. Prepare as directed on package, chilling thoroughly.

*For use with Pillsbury's Best Self-Rising Flour, omit salt.

Elegant chocolate and vanilla swirls mounted on a chocolate crust make this a courtly cheesecake. Notice the 8-hour chill time.

Royal Marble Cheesecake

    ¾ cup Pillsbury's Best All Purpose Flour*
    2 tablespoons sugar
    ¼ teaspoon salt
    ¼ cup butter or margarine
    1 package (6 oz.) or 1 cup semi-sweet
      chocolate pieces, melted

Filling
    3 packages (8 oz. each) cream cheese,
      softened
    1 cup sugar
    ¼ cup Pillsbury's Best All Purpose or
      Self-Rising Flour
    2 teaspoons vanilla
    6 eggs
    1 cup dairy sour cream

OVEN 400°   16 SERVINGS

In small mixing bowl, combine flour, sugar and salt. Cut in butter until particles are fine. Stir in 2 tablespoons of the melted chocolate pieces. Press onto bottom of 9 or 10-inch springform pan. Bake at 400° for 10 minutes. Blend 1¾ cups of Filling with the remaining melted chocolate pieces. Pour remainder of Filling over baked crust. Top with spoonfuls of chocolate mixture. Cut through batter (not crust) to marble. Place in 400° oven; immediately reduce setting to 300°. Bake 1 hour. Turn off oven; leave in closed oven 1 hour. Cool away from drafts until completely cooled. Chill at least 8 hours before serving.

Filling: In large mixer bowl, beat cream cheese with sugar at medium speed until smooth and creamy. Blend in flour and vanilla. Add eggs, one at a time, beating well after each. Blend in sour cream.
*For use with Pillsbury's Best Self-Rising Flour, omit salt.
*HIGH ALTITUDE ADJUSTMENT — 5,200 FEET.
Bake at 300° for 60 or 70 minutes.*

Soaring circles of pastry layered with coconut cream, all encased in an oven-browned meringue. Give yourself an hour plus time to cool.

Coconut Strata

1 package Pillsbury Pie Crust Mix or Sticks
Filling
    1 package (3¼ oz.) coconut cream pudding
      and pie filling mix
    2 cups milk
    8 tablespoons toasted coconut
Meringue
    3 egg whites
    ⅓ cup sugar

OVEN 450°   8 SERVINGS

Prepare pie crust mix or sticks as directed on package for double crust pastry. Divide into 4 equal portions. Flatten each into a circle ½-inch thick; smooth edges. Roll out each portion on floured surface to an 8-inch circle; cut around an inverted 8-inch pie pan to even edges. Transfer each to ungreased cookie sheet; prick generously with fork. Bake at 450° for 7 to 10 minutes until light brown. Cool. Place a pastry circle on plate or cookie sheet. Spoon ½ cup Filling over circle, spreading to within ¼ inch of edge; sprinkle with 2 tablespoons of coconut; top with another pastry circle. Continue to spread Filling; sprinkle coconut and stack layers. Spread remaining Filling on top pastry to within 1 inch of edge; sprinkle with coconut. Spread Meringue around sides and over uncovered edge of top pastry circle. Decorate center with a swirl of Meringue. Bake at 450° for 8 to 10 minutes until light brown. Cool before serving.

Filling: In saucepan, combine pudding mix and milk. Cook, stirring constantly, over medium heat until mixture comes to a full boil. Cool.
Meringue: In small mixer bowl, beat egg whites at high speed until soft mounds form. Gradually add sugar; continue beating until stiff, glossy peaks form.

Chilly chocolate filling made with whipped cream crowns a meringue baked in a pastry shell. Cinnamon makes it mysterious.

Chocolate Angel Strata

9-inch Baked Pastry Shell, see page 63

Meringue
   2 egg whites
  ½ teaspoon white vinegar
  ¼ teaspoon salt
  ¼ teaspoon cinnamon
  ½ cup sugar

Chocolate Whipped Cream Filling
  2 egg yolks, slightly beaten
  ¼ cup water
  1 cup (6 oz. package) semi-sweet
    chocolate pieces
  1 cup whipping cream
  ¼ cup sugar
  ¼ teaspoon cinnamon

OVEN 325°   9-INCH PIE

Meringue: In small mixer bowl, combine egg whites, vinegar, salt and cinnamon. Beat at high speed until foamy. Add sugar; beat at high speed until meringue stands in stiff peaks. Spread meringue on bottom and up sides of baked pastry shell. Bake at 325° for 15 to 18 minutes, until lightly browned. Cool.

Chocolate Whipped Cream Filling: In small saucepan, combine egg yolks, water and chocolate pieces. Cook over medium heat, stirring constantly, until chocolate is melted and mixture thickens. Cool. In small mixer bowl, combine whipping cream, sugar and cinnamon; beat until thickened. Blend in cooled chocolate mixture; spread over Meringue. Chill at least 4 hours before serving.

Spicy pumpkin cheesecake in a buttery crust. A new twist for fall and holiday entertaining and you can do it ahead.

Party Pumpkin Dessert

Crust
  1 cup Pillsbury's Best All Purpose Flour*
  ¼ cup sugar
  ½ teaspoon baking powder
  ¼ teaspoon salt
  ¼ cup butter or margarine, softened
  1 egg

Pumpkin-Cheese Filling
  1 package (8 oz.) cream cheese, softened
  ¾ cup firmly packed brown sugar
  1 teaspoon cinnamon
  1 teaspoon nutmeg
  ½ teaspoon salt
  ½ teaspoon ginger
  ¼ teaspoon cloves
  3 eggs
  1 can (1 lb.) or 1½ cups canned pumpkin
  1 cup light cream
  1 teaspoon vanilla

Sour Cream Topping
  1 cup dairy sour cream
  ¼ cup firmly packed brown sugar
  ½ teaspoon cinnamon
  ⅛ teaspoon ginger
  ⅛ teaspoon nutmeg
  1 teaspoon vanilla

OVEN 375°   12 TO 14 SERVINGS

Crust: In small mixer bowl, combine all Crust ingredients. Mix at low speed until well blended. With floured fingers, press mixture into bottom and 1½ inches up sides of ungreased 10-inch spring form or 9-inch square pan.

Pumpkin-Cheese Filling: In large mixer bowl, combine all filling ingredients. Mix at medium speed 2 minutes, until well blended. Pour into crust. Bake at 375° for 1 hour 15 minutes or until filling is set in the center. Spread on Sour Cream Topping and bake 15 minutes more. Cool completely. Chill at least 5 hours or overnight before serving.

Sour Cream Topping: In small mixing bowl, combine all Topping ingredients. Mix until well blended.

*For use with Pillsbury's Best Self-Rising Flour, omit baking powder and salt in crust.

Spectacular individual tarts filled with dark sweet cherries under a sophisticated sour cream topping. Prepare ahead; then put together at serving time.

Cherry Honeys

    1 package Pillsbury Pie Crust Mix or Sticks
    1 can (1 lb.) pitted dark sweet cherries,
       drain and reserve syrup
1½ tablespoons cornstarch
  ¼ cup honey
    1 tablespoon grated orange peel, if desired
    1 tablespoon lemon juice

<u>Sour Cream Topping</u>
  ½ cup whipping cream
  ½ cup flaked coconut
  ⅓ cup dairy sour cream
    2 tablespoons sugar

OVEN 450°   6 TO 8 SERVINGS

Prepare pie crust mix or sticks according to package directions for one-crust pie. Divide dough into 6 or 8 pieces. Roll each piece to a circle to fit into 3 or 4-inch tart pans or muffin cups. Fold edge to form a standing rim; flute. Prick generously. Bake at 450° for 8 to 10 minutes until golden brown. Cool.

In 2-quart saucepan, gradually add reserved syrup to cornstarch, stirring until smooth. Add honey and orange peel. Cook over medium heat, stirring constantly, until thick and clear. Add lemon juice and cherries; cool. Just before serving, spoon cherry filling into tart shells. Garnish with Sour Cream Topping.

<u>Sour Cream Topping</u>: In small mixer bowl, beat whipping cream until thick. Fold in coconut, sour cream and sugar.

<u>Tip:</u> *Scoops of vanilla ice cream may be substituted for Sour Cream Topping.*

Pineapple spears wrapped in crescent dough and baked on a stick. Kids will love to eat them.

Pineapple Stick Pops

    2 tablespoons firmly packed brown sugar
    1 tablespoon flour
  ½ teaspoon nutmeg
    8 canned pineapple spears, drained
    1 can Pillsbury Refrigerated Quick
       Crescent Dinner Rolls
    8 wooden skewers or popsicle sticks
    3 tablespoons caramel ice cream topping
      Nuts
      Flaked coconut

OVEN 375°   8 STICK POPS

Combine brown sugar, flour and nutmeg. Roll pineapple spears in sugar mixture. Separate crescent rolls. Place a pineapple spear along wide end of triangle; roll to point, folding in sides. Place on cookie sheet; insert wooden skewer. Repeat with remaining rolls. Bake at 375° for 15 to 20 minutes until golden brown. Cool. Drizzle with caramel topping; sprinkle with nuts or coconut.

Lower the lights to serve these extraordinary crepes drenched in orange-honey sauce and flamed with brandy. A wise hostess makes the pancakes well ahead of time.

Delicate Orange Crepes

    I cup creamed cottage cheese
    I cup dairy sour cream
    I tablespoon sugar
  ¾ teaspoon salt
    I tablespoon grated orange peel
    3 tablespoons orange juice
    4 eggs
    I cup Pillsbury's Best All Purpose Flour*
  ¼ cup brandy

Orange Honey Sauce

  ½ cup honey
  ⅓ cup butter or margarine
  ¼ teaspoon cinnamon
    2 teaspoons grated orange peel
    2 tablespoons orange juice

                    5 TO 6 SERVINGS

In electric blender container or in large mixer bowl, blend cottage cheese until very fine grained. Add sour cream, sugar, salt, orange peel, orange juice, eggs and flour; blend at high speed until well mixed. Heat a 5 to 6-inch skillet over medium high heat. Grease lightly before baking each crepe. Pour batter, scant ¼ cup at a time, into skillet, tilting pan to spread evenly over bottom. When crepe is light brown and set, turn to brown other side. Roll warm pancakes. Arrange on oblong serving dish or on individual serving plates, three or four on each. Pour hot Orange Honey Sauce over pancakes. Warm brandy in container with long handle just until small bubbles form; ignite with match. Immediately pour over pancakes. Serve with whipped cream, if desired.

Orange Honey Sauce: Blend all ingredients in saucepan. Cook over medium heat, stirring occasionally, until hot.

Tip: Crepes may be made ahead of time, stored in refrigerator or freezer. Reheat by covering and placing in 350° oven for 15 minutes. Roll and serve.

*For use with Pillsbury's Best Self-Rising Flour, omit salt.

Walnuts, cinnamon and apricot preserves are layered between a rich no-rise yeast dough, finished with a flourish with a baked meringue topping.

Streamlined Hungarian Torte

    1 package active dry yeast
    ¼ cup warm water
    1⅓ cups butter, softened
    3½ cups Pillsbury's Best All Purpose or
        Self-Rising Flour
    4 egg yolks
    ½ cup dairy sour cream
    1½ cups chopped walnuts
    ¾ cup sugar
    1 teaspoon cinnamon
    1 jar (10 oz.) or 1 cup apricot preserves
    ¼ cup chopped walnuts

Meringue Topping
    4 egg whites
    ½ cup sugar

OVEN 350°   14 TO 16 SERVINGS

Soften yeast in water. In large mixer bowl, combine butter and flour at low speed until mixture resembles coarse crumbs. Add egg yolks, sour cream and softened yeast. Blend at low speed until a dough forms. Shape into a ball. Divide into 3 portions.

Roll out each portion of dough on floured surface to 13x9-inch rectangles. Place one rectangle in bottom of greased 13x9-inch pan. Combine 1½ cups walnuts, sugar and cinnamon; sprinkle over dough in pan. Top with second rectangle of dough; spread with preserves. Top with remaining dough. Bake at 350° for 50 to 55 minutes. Cover with Meringue Topping; sprinkle with ¼ cup chopped walnuts. Continue baking 10 to 15 minutes or until Meringue is golden brown. Cool. Serve cut in squares.

Meringue Topping: Beat egg whites until soft peaks form. Gradually add sugar; continue beating until stiff peaks form.

Tip: If desired, other flavors of preserves may be substituted for apricot preserves.

A yeast dough crust goes continental with a cheese filling that smacks of pineapple and coconut. Serve in squares, warm or cold. Allow plenty of time for rising.

Pastry Shop Cheese Slices

    1 package active dry yeast
¼ cup warm water
    1 tablespoon sugar
½ cup butter or margarine, softened
    2 cups Pillsbury's Best All Purpose or
       Self-Rising Flour
    1 egg
½ teaspoon vanilla

Pineapple Filling

    3 tablespoons sugar
    2 tablespoons flour
⅛ teaspoon salt
    1 can (13¼ oz.) crushed pineapple,
       undrained

Cheese Filling

    2 eggs
¾ cup sugar
    2 tablespoons flour
    1 teaspoon vanilla
    2 cups (1 pint) creamed small curd
       cottage cheese
    1 package (8 oz.) cream cheese, softened
½ cup flaked coconut

Glaze

    1 cup confectioners' sugar
    2 tablespoons milk
½ teaspoon vanilla

OVEN 375°   12 TO 14 SERVINGS

Soften yeast in water. In large mixer bowl, combine sugar, butter and flour; blend at low speed until mixture is crumbly. Add softened yeast, egg and vanilla. Mix at low speed until a dough forms. Roll out two-thirds of dough on floured surface to 16x12-inch rectangle. Place in bottom of greased 13x9-inch pan, pressing dough up sides of pan. Spread Pineapple Filling over dough. Carefully spread on Cheese Filling. Roll out remaining dough to a 13x9-inch rectangle. Carefully place over Filling. Fold bottom crust over top to seal edges. Cover; let rise in warm place until light, about 1 hour. Flute edge. Bake at 375° for 30 to 35 minutes until golden brown. While warm, spread with Glaze. Cool. Refrigerate until served.

Pineapple Filling: In small saucepan, combine sugar, flour, salt and pineapple. Cook over medium heat, stirring constantly, until thickened. Remove from heat; cool.

Cheese Filling: In large mixer bowl, combine eggs, sugar, flour and vanilla. Beat at medium speed until thick. Add cottage cheese, cream cheese and coconut; beat at medium speed until well blended.

Glaze: In small mixer bowl, combine all ingredients; blend until smooth.

Individual molded pudding cakes, turned out of custard cups, feature an apricot perched on a custard pudding, with a sponge cake base. Make ahead and chill until your guests arrive.

Spun Gold Apricot Dessert

¾ cup sugar
½ cup Pillsbury's Best All Purpose Flour*
½ teaspoon salt
    2 tablespoons butter or margarine,
       softened
    1 can (12 oz.) or 1½ cups apricot nectar
    1 tablespoon lemon juice
    3 eggs, separated
¼ cup sugar
    1 can (1 lb. 1 oz.) unpeeled apricot
       halves, drained

OVEN 325°   9 SERVINGS

In large mixer bowl, combine ¾ cup sugar, flour, salt, butter, apricot nectar, lemon juice and egg yolks at lowest speed; beat for 1 minute at medium speed.

Beat egg whites until soft peaks form. Gradually add ¼ cup sugar, beating until stiff peaks form. Gently fold into batter.

Arrange apricot halves in 9 greased 6-oz. custard cups. Fill each custard cup three-fourths full with batter. Place cups in pan of hot water. Bake at 325° for 45 to 55 minutes until golden brown. Cool. Invert onto serving plates; serve with whipped cream if desired.

*Self-Rising Flour is not recommended for use in this recipe.

Index